Three E

CW00949791

THREE BUDO MASTERS

Jigoro Kano (Judo)
•
Gichin Funakoshi (Karate)
•
Morihei Ueshiba (Aikido)

by
John Stevens

KODANSHA INTERNATIONAL
Tokyo • New York • London

Distributed in the United States by Kodansha America, Inc., 114 Fifth Avenue, New York N.Y. 10011, and in the United Kingdom and continental Europe by Kodansha Europe Ltd., 95 Aldwych, London WC2B 4JF. Published by Kodansha International Ltd., 17-14 Otowa 1-chome, Bunkyo-ku, Tokyo 112, and Kodansha America, Inc.

95 96 97 10 9 8 7 6 5 4 3 2 1

ISBN 4-7700-1852-5

Contents

Preface

Three Budo Masters is a presentation of the lives and teachings of Jigoro Kano (1860–1938), the sophisticated internationalist who founded Kodokan Judo; Gichin Funakoshi (1868–1957), a cultured gentleman scholar who is reckoned as the father of modern karate; and Morihei Ueshiba (1883–1969), the mystic sage who created aikido. The three *budo* (martial art) masters were well acquainted with each other, and the men and their students interacted in a variety of fascinating ways. Their respective teachings had a profound impact on modern Japanese society, and practice of the arts of judo, karate, and aikido spread quickly to other lands. All three arts are now avidly studied all over the globe, an integral part of world culture.

Popularization of any art always includes certain dangers, however, and all three masters would undoubtedly be sorely dismayed at the changes that have taken place in the world of budo: increasing commercialization, excessive emphasis on competition, vicious factional disputes, and scandalous behavior by senior instructors. Kano, Funakoshi, and Ueshiba were men of vision who held the loftiest ideals and maintained the highest standards; it is my sincere hope that *Three Budo Masters* will stimulate a reassessment of the real nature and true purpose of judo, karate, and aikido.

John Stevens
Sendai, 1995

Jigoro Kano

(1860–1938)

SHUT OFF FROM THE WORLD FOR MORE THAN two centuries by the Tokugawa Shoguns, Japan's long isolation ended on March 31, 1854, with the signing of the Treaty of Kanagawa. The old order in Japan quickly crumbled as the island nation prepared to meet the world. It was a period of stupendous change and immense challenge; the entire political and economic landscape of Japan would be transformed within a few decades. Just as this new era was dawning in Japan, Jigoro Kano was born on October 28, 1860 in Mikage.

Overlooking placid Osaka Bay and backed by the majestic Rokko mountain range, Mikage (now part of Kobe City) was then one of the most pleasant areas of Western Japan. The region is blessed with a temperate climate and pure water, two resources put to good use in sake brewing, still one of the primary industries of the district. On his father's (Mareshiba's) side, the family line stretched back to the beginnings of Japanese history, and Kano's ancestors include many illustrious Shinto priests, Buddhist masters, and Confucian scholars. His mother, Sadako, came from one of the main sake brewing clans (they produced the renowned Kiku-Masamune brand). Kano, together with two older brothers and two older sisters, grew up in a home that was among the largest and best appointed in the neighborhood.

While Kano's early circumstances were enviable, his upbringing was strict and disciplined. Kano had fond memories of a kind and considerate mother, but he also remembered her as someone who would not tolerate any kind of improper behavior. Mareshiba took personal charge of his youngest son's education, instructing him in the basics, and arranged for additional tutoring in the Chinese classics and calligraphy.

Following Sadako's death in 1869, Mareshiba, who had become an entrepreneur and government official actively promoting the modernization of Meiji Japan, moved the family to the new capital of Tokyo. The young Kano's most vivid first impression of the capital was the sight of *ronin* swaggering along the streets and proudly displaying their two swords. (The prohibition against wearing swords was enacted some months after the Kano family arrived in Tokyo.) Kano was enrolled in the Seitatsu Shojuku, a private academy operated by the scholar Keido Ubukata. This academy was unique in that it accepted not only the offspring of aristocrats and samurai (heretofore learning was exclusively a privilege of the upper classes) but also numbered among its students children of merchants, craftsmen, restaurateurs, and others, some of whom were in training to be sumo wrestlers, kabuki actors, and geisha. Ubukata was a highly regarded calligrapher as well as a scholar, and in addition to drilling his pupils in the classics of China and Japan, he made each student submit, daily, three notebooks full of sample brushwork. In the evenings after classes, Ubukata often held informal discussions on contemporary affairs, and he told Kano that while a classical education was invaluable, from now on Japanese students needed to acquaint themselves thoroughly with Western culture as well.

Taking Ubukata's advice to heart, Kano initially studied English at the academy of Shubei Mitsukuri, and then, in 1873, he entered the Ikuei Gijuku, where all the courses were taught in English or German by foreign instructors (the mathematics textbook was in Dutch). In the dormitory attached to the school, the brilliant, well-bred (and somewhat snobbish) Kano was subject to severe hazing by jealous seniors, against whom he was defenseless. Kano naturally regretted this sorry state of affairs, and it was during this troublesome period that he first heard of *jujutsu*, the martial art that enabled a softer physical force to control a hard attack. Kano was not able to practice jujutsu until later, but he did try to build up his body by engaging in various sports, including the newly introduced game of baseball.

In 1874 Kano entered the Tokyo School of Foreign Languages, where he had to learn English all over again. His previous English teachers had been Dutch or German, and when faced with British and American native pronunciation he was at a total loss. Kano's assiduous study of English under difficult conditions was remarkable. Not only were dictionaries scarce in those days, but the students at the academy were often obliged to share a single textbook. Prior to exams, Kano's "textbook shift" was sometimes from 1:00 A.M. to 5:00 A.M. Despite such obstacles, Kano mastered the language, keeping a diary in English most of his adult life. (Later Kano was to write his budo technical notes in English as well, probably to keep them secret. His English penmanship was outstanding, admired as among the finest in Japan.) After graduating from the Language School, Kano entered the Kaisei Academy, another government sponsored school. In 1877 the Academy became Tokyo University, and Kano had the honor of being a member of the first freshman class of the nation's premier educational institution. He declared his majors to be political science, philosophy, and literature. (His favorite subject turned out to be astronomy.) During this period Kano once again found himself confronted by bullies and ruffians both on and off campus, and he became more determined than ever to practice jujutsu. At that particular moment in history, however, it was not easy to find a suitable teacher.

During the Tokugawa period (1600–1868), each domain in Japan employed martial arts instructors as a matter of course and every samurai man and woman received extensive training in *bujutsu*. However, once the feudal system collapsed in 1868, government support for martial art academies ceased, and most were forced to close. Furthermore, with the increasing Westernization of the country, most Japanese lost interest in the classical martial arts. "Times have changed and such things are no longer use-

•

•

ful," Kano was bluntly admonished, not only by his father but even by many former martial artists.

Kano persisted, and finally in 1877 he located a good instructor, Hachinosuke Fukuda (1829–80), of the Tenshin Shin'yo Ryu. This Ryu, established by Mataemon Iso (d. 1862), was a comparatively new style of jujutsu, emphasizing *atemi* (strikes to anatomical weak points) and grappling techniques. It is said that Mataemon learned many of his tactics in the street, fighting off groups of rogues who terrorized the populace (law and order had largely broken down near the end of the Shogunate). He supposedly knew 124 different types of punches.

The fifty-year-old Fukuda, who made a living as a chiropractor, had a small dojo with few regular students. Nevertheless, Kano threw himself wholeheartedly into the training, and if no one else showed up he practiced alone, executing various movements with a heavy iron rod Fukuda had given him. (It seems that Kano also briefly studied *bojutsu*, stick fighting, at a Yagyu Shingen Ryu dojo around this time.) Kano constantly covered his aching body with a potent but foul-smelling salve of his own concoction and thus quickly became known among his classmates as "Kano the Odoriferous." Every night, returning home, he would demonstrate for his older brother and sister what he had learned at Fukuda's dojo during the day.

During the lessons, the eager Kano pestered Fukuda for a detailed explanation of every technique—the exact placement of the hands and feet, the correct angle of entry, the proper distribution of weight, and so on—but the mas-

The young, vigorous, and keenly focused Jigoro Kano in his jujutsu training days. Kano had three principal jujutsu teachers: Hachinosuke Fukuda and Masamoto Iso of the Tenshin Shin'yo Ryu, and Tsunetoshi Iikubo of the Kito Ryu. He also studied Western arts such as wrestling and boxing. Based on practical experience and theoretical studies, Kano founded Kodokan Judo in 1882. (All photographs of Kano courtesy of the Kodokan.)

ter would usually just say, "Come here," and throw Kano repeatedly, until the inquisitive student gained practical knowledge of the technique through first-hand experience.

Kano's main training partner was a powerful heavyweight named Fukushima. Since Fukushima stymied Kano in *randori* (free-style competition), Kano asked a sumo wrestler friend for advice, hoping that sumo techniques would improve his performance. Sumo was of no help, however, so Kano visited the Tokyo Library to see what books on Western wrestling had to offer. There he discovered a technique he later called *kata-guruma* (shoulder wheel), which he employed on Fukushima with good results.

In May 1879 Kano and Fukushima were among a select group of martial artists chosen to stage a demonstration for former United States president U. S. Grant when he visited Japan. The demonstration was favorably received by General Grant and his party, and widely reported in the American press. Unfortunately, Kano's teacher, Fukuda, died not long after that demonstration at the age of fifty-two. Kano attempted to keep the dojo in operation by himself, but soon realized that he needed more training.

Kano thus continued his study of the Tenshin Shin'yo Ryu with Masamoto Iso (1818–81), son of the school's founder. Since Masamoto was in his sixties at the time he no longer engaged in *randori*, but he was still considered a master of *kata*, techniques practiced in arranged patterns. (Kano later told his own students that Masamoto's *kata*

•

17

•

were "the most beautiful I ever saw executed.") Masamoto also possessed a cast-iron frame, able to withstand a direct blow to the body made with a wooden sword. Kano gained proficiency in various *kata* under Masamoto's tutelage, and acquired extensive experience in *randori* as well; there were thirty students in Masamoto's dojo, and Kano would have matches with all of them before the end of the day. Often he would not finish training until 11:00 P.M., and not infrequently was overcome by fatigue on the way home. When he did manage to make it home, Kano re-fought the matches in his sleep, punching holes with his hands and feet in the paper doors of his room.

As Kano grew stronger and increasingly skilled, his confidence grew. At a demonstration given by the Totsuka Ryu at Tokyo University, Kano impetuously leaped from the audience and joined in the *randori*, impressing both participants and onlookers with his impromptu perfor-mance. On the other hand, Kano discovered that overcon-fidence can be dangerous when, at Masamoto's dojo, he once sloppily applied a throw and was nearly pinned by a rank beginner. After that close call, Kano learned never to take anyone for granted.

In 1881, when Masamoto died, Kano was once more left without a teacher. This time he went to train with Tsunetoshi Iikubo (1835–89) of the Kito Ryu. The pedi-gree of the Kito Ryu dates back to the mid-seventeenth century. While the identity of the original founder of the school is in dispute, the Kito tradition was influenced by the teachings of the Yagyu School and those of Zen Mas-ter Takuan (1573–1645), lending it a more philosophical cast than that of the pragmatic Tenshin Shin'yo Ryu. In Kano's time the Kito Ryu focused primarily on *nage-waza*, throwing techniques. In both style and content the Kito Ryu curriculum differed considerably from that of the Tenshin Shin'yo Ryu, and Kano was pleased to be exposed to another perspective on jujutsu. Although already in his fifties, Iikubo continued to train full-time, and he could still best his young students in *randori*. He was likely the most skilled martial artist under whom Kano trained. (In his memoirs Kano stated, "From Master Fukuda, I learned what my life's work would be; from Master Masamoto, I learned the subtle nature of *kata*; and from Master Iikubo, I learned varied techniques and the importance of timing.")

While training in jujutsu during the evenings, Kano pored over his books just as hard during the day, achieving outstanding marks at Tokyo University. One of his principal professors there was Ernest Fenollosa (1853–1908). (At that time twenty-seven of thirty-nine professors at Tokyo University were Westerners.) Although hired as a professor of Western philosophy, Fenollosa became infatuated with Oriental culture and tirelessly promoted the study of Asian fine arts among both Westerners and the Japanese themselves. In the early Meiji period, there was a danger that the Japanese, in their headlong rush to modernize and emulate the West, would abandon their own culture. Pens, for example, had replaced the brush in art school classes. Fenollosa warned against such mindless adoption of Western practices, and convinced his friends and students (including Kano) that traditional Japanese arts were vital forms well worth preserving.

Another of Kano's favorite professors was the eccentric Zen priest Tanzan Hara (1819–1931), who taught Indian philosophy. Hara had little use for the trappings of religion, a view Kano came to share, and has been immortalized in modern Zen literature as the hero of this oft-repeated tale:

> Two novice monks, Tanzan and Ekido, were on a pilgrimage from one training monastery to another. A storm blew up, and the pair come to a crossroad that had been transformed into a fast flowing stream. A lovely young girl was stranded there. Tanzan inquired, "Do you need help?" When the girl replied "Yes," he gathered her up in his arms, carried her across the flooded road, and deposited her safely on the other side. After the two monks walked a bit further, Ekido suddenly burst out, "How could you do such a thing? You know it is strictly prohibited for Buddhist monks to touch women!" Tanzan shot back, "What? Are you still carrying that girl? I put her down long ago."

Kano graduated from Tokyo University in 1881 and stayed on another year for further study. In February of 1882 he moved to Eisho-ji, a small Jodo Sect Buddhist temple in the Shimo-tani section of Tokyo. There, at the precocious age of twenty-two, he founded the Kodokan, "Institute for Study of the Way."

Kano had fallen in love with jujutsu and believed that

•

•

it must be preserved as a Japanese cultural treasure; however, he also believed it had to be adapted to modern times. The underlying principles of jujutsu, he felt, should be systematized as Kodokan Judo, a discipline of the mind and body that fostered wisdom and virtuous living. Comparing jujutsu to Hinayana Buddhism, a small vehicle with limited vision, he equated Kodokan Judo to Mahayana Buddhism, a big vehicle that embraced both individuals and society as a whole. "If the work of a human being does not benefit society," he declared, "that person's existence is in vain." As for the term *judo*, the "way of softness," it had been in use for several hundred years. Several old texts, for instance, defined judo as the "path that follows the flow of things," which in Kodokan Judo Kano interpreted as the "most efficient use of energy."

Kano and his handful of students (nine officially enrolled that first year) practiced initially in a corner of the main temple hall. Soon, however, the severity of the training began to take a toll on the building—floorboards were shattered, memorial tablets on the altar tumbled to the floor, and roof tiles were dislodged—so an adjoining room was expanded into a separate twelve-mat dojo. Kano's teacher Iikubo visited the dojo once or twice a week to give instruction. Meanwhile, Kano was hired as a full-time instructor at Gakushuin, the Peers' School, in August of 1882 and launched on his parallel career as a professional educator.

During the first days of the Kodokan, Kano took in a fellow named Shirai to accommodate one of his father's friends. Shirai was a former military man, nice enough when sober but violent and difficult to control when he had had a few drinks. Each time Shirai became abusive, Kano would pin him, "gently and kindly," and wait patiently for him to calm down. Gradually Shirai learned to gain some control over his drinking, convincing Kano of the value of a gentle and kind judo.

In 1883 Kano moved to new quarters twice. The first move was to Minami Jimbo-cho, where he opened an English academy. The storehouse that was attached to the property he used as a dojo. Since it was inconvenient for most students to attend training during the week, the dojo was kept open on Sunday from 7:00 A.M to 12:00 noon and from 3:00 P.M to 7:00 P.M. As instructor, Kano had to be continually on hand, even if it was freezing cold (the storehouse was unheated) and no students showed up. A few months later he moved to Kami Niban-cho in Kojimachi and built a small dojo on the grounds of his rented residence. The dojo was open every afternoon from 2:00 P.M. to 11:00 or 12:00 at night. Kano would come out to teach when anyone came to train.

Iikubo continued to teach Kano during the first half of 1883, dominating his student as usual. Then, one day, Kano grasped the key to judo—"If my partner pulls, I push; if he pushes, I pull." Thereafter he was able to compete on equal terms. Kano ascribed this breakthrough not to any mystical experience, as was often the case with martial artists of the past, but rather to the result of years of careful investigation and a rational approach to the art. Although Iikubo bestowed a Kito Ryu teaching license on him in the autumn of 1883, Kano still had a hard time at-

•

22

•

tracting students owing to his youth and a lack of proper training facilities.

Only eight students formally registered in 1883, and ten the following year. In 1884 Kano was able to construct a larger dojo (though still only twenty mats in size) and establish regular days of open competition. A ranking system gradually came into being—at this incipient stage, three basic levels (*kyu*) and three advanced ranks (*dan*). Jojiro Tomita (1865–1937) and Shiro Saigo (1866–1922) were the first two trainees to be presented with the rank of *shodan*. Around this time, Kano also instituted *kan-geiko*, "cold weather training," thirty days of special mid-winter practice between four and seven in the morning.

During this period, the regimen of a live-in student at the Kodokan—most of whom Kano supported entirely out of his own pocket—was as austere as that of any monk. A live-in student had to rise at 4:45 A.M. and immaculately clean his room, the buildings, and the grounds. The day was strictly divided into periods of book study (philosophy, political science, economics, and psychology) and judo training. While studying, the trainee had to wear a kimono with *hakama* (pleated pants) and sit in *seiza*. When not training or studying, he was kept busy looking after guests, cooking meals, and preparing the bath. The day ended at 9:30 P.M.

Kano and the students met for tea once a week, and there was a long outdoor walk scheduled each Sunday afternoon. The motto of Kano's academy was "Do it yourself," and all students were responsible for washing and mending their uniforms. Kano's own schedule was much the same, with the added burden of often sitting up all night to do translation work for the Ministry of Education in order to make ends meet.

While undertaking a simultaneous investigation of Western sports such as wrestling and boxing, Kano continued his research into the classical budo systems of Japan. Being only slightly older than the trainees, he practiced just as intently as they did. Shiro Saigo, who had received training in the secret *oshiki-uchi* techniques of Aizu samurai prior to joining the Kodokan, was one student who quickly learned how to counter the throws of his teacher. In the end, Kano was forced continually to refine the Kodokan techniques based on both his practical experience and theoretical studies. Looking back on these early days of the Kodokan, one sees that the primary emphasis was on throws, and that the most dangerous techniques were gradually eliminated from *randori*.

During this period Kano was also practicing judo a lot outside of the dojo. He was obliged to use a horse often in those days to get around, but he never really got the hang of horseback riding. Thanks to his judo breakfall training, however, he learned to land safely on his feet each time a horse threw him.

By 1885 the number of applicants had increased to fifty-four, and even some foreigners began to ask for instruction. The first non-Japanese trainees were apparently two brothers named Eastlake from the United States. (They did not last long, but in 1899 were succeeded by a Professor Ladd from Princeton University, who spent ten months of serious training at the Kodokan.) In 1886 Kano moved his residence again, this time to Fujimi-cho, where he was able to build a nice forty-mat facility—ninety-nine students registered that year. At the Fujimi-cho dojo students with *dan* rankings first began wearing black belts as a sign of their status.

Over the next few years members of the Kodokan began to distinguish themselves in open tournaments sponsored by the National Police Agency. The glorious victories have become part of Kodokan Judo mythology, but there are so many discrepancies in the various accounts that it is not really certain where, when, and against whom the matches were fought. Similarly, Saigo is feted for having achieved a resounding victory with his *yama-arashi* ("mountain-storm") technique, but it is not clear exactly what this technique was. It is said by some that *yama-arashi* describes Saigo's style—"like a fierce wind howling down a mountain peak"—rather than a particular throw. Also, it appears that the rules of these tournaments may have favored Kodokan competitors, since the most lethal techniques of the old-style schools were prohibited. (Heretofore, open contests had been deadly serious; as a precaution, competitors in such battles bid farewell to their parents and friends before setting off to join the fray.) There is no question, however, that the Kodokan members did distinguish themselves in these tournaments and in many other open challenges over the coming years.

While Kodokan members usually acquitted themselves quite well, they were by no means invincible. One of the most powerful of Kodokan trainees was Sanbo Toku (1886–1945), who refused to learn how to take breakfalls because "no one will ever be able to throw me." That may have been true at the Kodokan and among street fighters (Toku once took on a group of Brazilian sailors), but when Toku challenged Zenmi Kunii (d. 1930) of the Kajima Shin Ryu, he was tossed about "like a kitten." Other masters unbowed by Kodokan challengers included Morikichi Omori (1853–1930), swashbuckling master of the Yoshin Totsuka Ryu, who defeated all comers with his irresistible *kiai jutsu* (a kind of martial art mesmerism), and Mataemon Tanabe (1851–1928), a slight, dignified man who learned how to pin his opponents by "practicing catching eels with my bare hands and watching snakes swallow frogs." A number of old-style jujutsu schools banded together as the Shindo Rokugo Kai in opposition to Kodokan Judo, but that organization was simply no match for Kano's carefully thought-out and well-planned system.

In April of 1888, Kano, together with the Rev. T. Lindsay, delivered a paper (and presumably a demonstration) on "Jujutsu" to the members of the Asiatic Society of Japan, a study group consisting of English-speaking foreign diplomats, professors, and businessmen. In the paper, the authors contended that while there is evidence of certain Japanese martial arts being influenced by Chinese boxing, jujutsu is purely of native origin. The paper illustrated the principle of *ju* by relating the tale of an old-time teacher observing willow branches yielding, but not breaking, under the weight of heavy snow. It also contained stories of famous masters of jujutsu, including that of Jushin Sekiguchi (1597–1670). One day while Sekiguchi was accompanying his lord across a narrow bridge,

•

•

the lord decided to test the jujutsu master by suddenly driving him to the edge. Sekiguchi seemed to yield but at the last second slipped around and had to save the lord from being catapulted head-first into the water.

By 1889, when Kano relocated again to the Kami-Ni-bancho area, he had more than 1,500 full-time students and several branches of the Kodokan in different parts of Tokyo. Kano's Kodokan Judo was on its way to assuming a preeminent position in the martial art world of modern Japan.

In August of 1889 Kano resigned his position at Gakushuin and, at the request of the Imperial Household Agency, prepared to embark on a long inspection tour of educational institutions in Europe. Leaving his senior disciples, Saigo and Tomita, in charge of the Kodokan and accompanied by another official of the Imperial Household Agency, he set sail from Yokohama on September 15, 1889. With few people from Japan traveling overseas at that time, Kano and his companion found themselves the only Japanese passengers on board.

After stopping in Shanghai, they arrived in Marseilles in October. Over the next year, Kano visited Lyons, Paris, Brussels, Berlin, Vienna, Copenhagen, Stockholm, Amsterdam, the Hague, Rotterdam, and London, and on the return trip he stopped at Cairo to view the Pyramids. During the trip Kano was most impressed by the large number of huge churches and cathedrals, and at first he believed religion to be a pervasive force in European society. After talking with the Europeans themselves and observing their behavior, however, he concluded that while religion may

•

•

once have held sway, that was no longer the case.

Kano was further impressed with the frugality of many Europeans, who were careful not to waste anything. Seeing this virtue practiced in foreign lands reaffirmed one of Kano's principal beliefs: in judo as well as in daily life, one should always strive for the most efficient use of objects and energy. He also noted that while Japanese students who studied foreign languages were hesitant to speak or write for fear of committing a blunder, native speakers often garbled their syntax and sent him letters full of spelling mistakes. This was not the ideal, of course, but it did prove to Kano that Japanese students should not be overly concerned about making errors when learning to speak or write a foreign language. All in all, Kano enjoyed his first visit to Europe very much, and he felt that Japanese and Europeans were capable of associating on friendly terms.

Having visited Egypt in the company of an Englishman, a Frenchman, a Dutchman, a Swiss, and an Austrian, Kano proudly reported to his friends back in Japan that he alone was able to race to the top of a pyramid and back down without requiring any assistance or a break for water. During the long return voyage, Kano discussed judo with his follow passengers and demonstrated its efficacy. There being a strongman Russian sailor on board, a challenge match was arranged for want of better entertainment. Even though the sailor got a good grip on Kano, the judo master was able to improvise a technique—"half *koshi-nage*, half *seoi-nage*"—and throw his opponent. What impressed the crowd of passengers most was not the

•

28

•

ability of the smaller man to throw the larger, but the fact that Kano held the big sailor in a manner that kept him from being injured when he hit the deck.

While the ship was docked in Saigon, Kano took a stroll through the city. On the outskirts of town he was suddenly surrounded by a pack of wild dogs. His first impulse was to try to fight them off, but as he regained his composure, he found that the dogs also quieted down, and as a result he was able to pass through the pack unharmed.

Kano returned to Japan in mid-January 1891. He had been abroad for sixteen months. Unfortunately, Saigo had gotten into trouble in the meantime. As mentioned above, during these early years some Kodokan members continued to visit rival schools in order to test their skill. Among them was Saigo, who, along with some of his non-Kodokan jujutsu pals, had taken to loitering near busy market places and challenging all comers. One day Saigo and his gang were confronted by a group of sumo wrestlers, headed by the behemoth Araumi, "Stormy Sea." Araumi made short work of the other jujutsu men, leaving Saigo to meet the challenge. Though tipsy with *sake*, Saigo managed to down his man. When the big wrestler then proceeded to sink his teeth deep into Saigo's shin, the diminutive jujutsu man began to pummel him. A free-for-all among the sumo wrestlers and jujutsu men quickly ensued, the police were summoned, and the entire party hauled off to jail. To complicate matters, Saigo had injured several police officers during the melee. The other members of the Kodokan were able to get Saigo released from detention, but when Kano was informed of the incident he had no choice but to banish his most talented student for "infractions against the rules of the Kodokan." Saigo fled to distant Nagasaki, where he abandoned both jujutsu and judo. (In Nagasaki, Saigo took up *kyudo*, Japanese archery, and mastered that discipline just as thoroughly as he had jujutsu. In a gesture of forgiveness, upon Saigo's death Kano posthumously awarded his wayward former disciple the rank of "Kodokan Judo Sixth *Dan*.")

In 1891 the thirty-one-year-old Kano decided it was time to marry, and after seeking an appropriate match with the help of senior acquaintances, he wed Sumako Takezoe in August. Alas, Kano was obliged to leave his new bride behind in Tokyo the following month when he assumed the position of principal of the Fifth Higher School in remote Kumamoto.

As is always the case, educational innovation lagged behind in the provinces, and Kano viewed his job at the Fifth Higher School as a special challenge. The budget was meager, the facilities poor, and the teachers insufficiently trained. And neither was there a dojo. Without sufficient funds to build one, Kano and his students were forced to practice out-of-doors. Later, when the school was able to erect a dojo, Kano was joined by several of his disciples from Tokyo to help spread Kodokan Judo in southern Japan.

One of the new teachers hired at the school—reportedly at Kano's personal request although it is not clear how they first met—was Lafcadio Hearn (1850–1904). Hearn wrote an essay on "Jujutsu" that appeared in his book *Out of the East*, first published in 1892. The rambling essay says very little about Kano or judo, but it does make the point that Japan should rely on the spirit of judo—flexible yet firm—when dealing with Western powers. In his memoirs Kano mentions a rather elaborate ceremony held in town for which all of the participants were decked out in Western-style frock coats, dresses, or military uniforms save one person dressed totally Japanese-style—Lafcadio Hearn.

In 1893 Kano returned to Tokyo where he became principal of the First Higher School, and then, a bit later, he was appointed to the same position at the Tokyo Higher Normal School. He rejoined his wife, Sumako, and at the end of the year their first child, a daughter, was born. The couple went on to have eight children in all, five girls and three boys. The following year a nice hundred-mat dojo was built in Shimo Tomizaka-cho, and for the first time a small monthly fee was charged for lessons. (During Kano's lifetime the training fee at the Kodokan remained quite reasonable, thanks to the support of many generous patrons.)

It was also in 1894 that the Sino-Japanese war broke out. The subsequent war fever—which Kano did nothing to encourage—made the practice of judo more popular. During this period the "Food Bandit" incident occurred. For several nights running, an intruder broke into the Kodokan and pilfered the food supplies of the live-in trainees. Two students were posted as guards, but when they encountered the bandit, who was decked out in the guise of a Chinese *ninja*, they were severely beaten. After thrashing the pair the bandit sneered, "You pathetic weak-

•

lings! Don't you have anyone better to put on guard?" Upon receiving a report of that night's alarming events, the senior members of the dojo were nonplussed. If it took four or five Kodokan men to subdue a single bandit, it would make their judo look bad, so they decided to ask Sakujiro Yokoyama (1862–1912) to defend the honor of the Kodokan. Renowned for his devastating *tengu-nage* and nicknamed the "Demon," Yokoyama once fought a match against a jujutsu champion named Nakamura that lasted fifty-five minutes before the Metropolitan Chief of Police intervened to have the contest declared a draw.

That night, as anticipated, the bandit dropped from the ceiling and an epic battle ensued. Whoever the bandit was, he certainly knew his Chinese boxing, but Yokoyama held his own. Neither man could claim victory, but the bandit never returned to challenge Yokoyama or anyone else at the Kodokan again.

In 1895 the first version of the *gokyo no waza*, the five groups of instruction, were officially introduced at the Kodokan. Each group consisted of eight representative techniques—leg sweeps, throws, and body drops. In 1896 *shochu-geiko* was formally instituted—that is to say, "midsummer training," the steamy counterpart to the frigid "mid-winter training" already in force.

During this year Kano began lecturing regularly on the Three Elements of Judo, which might be summarized as follows:

•

•

Judo as Physical Education

The aim of physical education, Kano taught, is to make the body "strong, useful, and healthy." Further, physical education should train all of the muscles of the body in a systematic manner. It was lamentable, Kano argued, that most sports usually only train a certain set of muscles and neglect the others. As a result, physical imbalances occur. Kano devised a special set of warm-up exercises for judo practitioners that built up the entire body. Moreover, in regular training both *kata* and *randori* were utilized. *Kata*, to be practiced from both the left and right, inculcate the fundamentals of attack and defence. *Randori*, on the other hand, is freestyle training. In both cases, all the movements are to be executed according to the principle of *seiryoku zen'yo*, the "maximum efficient use of power."

Judo as a Sport

Randori is the basis of judo competition, the sporting element of Kano's system. Lethal moves are prohibited and the two competitors attempt to score a clean victory through good technique, maximum-efficient use of energy, and proper timing. *Randori* is, furthermore, a test of one's progress in the art, allowing the student to see how well he or she can do against other practitioners. While *randori* is important, Kano made it clear that competition is only

•

•

one aspect of the Kodokan Judo system, and it must not be over-emphasized.

Judo as Ethical Training

Training in Kodokan Judo, Kano believed, would help make one more alert, more confident, more decisive, and more focused. More importantly, Kodokan Judo was seen as providing one with a framework for learning how to apply Kano's other essential principle, *jita kyoei*, "mutual aid and co-operation." Applied in society, the principles of Kodokan Judo—diligence, flexibility, economy, good manners, and ethical behavior—would be of great benefit to all.

In his lectures, Kano also stressed the Five Principles of Judo in daily life:

1. Careful observation of oneself and one's situation, careful observation of others, and careful observation of the total environment.
2. Seize the initiative in whatever you undertake.
3. Consider fully, act decisively.
4. Know when to stop.
5. Keep to the middle, between elation and depression, exhaustion and sloth, foolhardiness and cowardly behavior.

The subsequent expansion of Kodokan Judo, at home and abroad, continued apace over the next three decades.

During these years Kano had a full schedule as head of the Kodokan, principal of the Tokyo Higher Normal School, member of a number of important government advisory committees, and, from 1909, the first and principal Japanese delegate to the International Olympic Committee. (On top of all this, Kano was elected to the House of Peers in 1922.) While he continued to lecture on, and give demonstrations of, Kodokan Judo throughout his life, he did very little actual training from his mid-thirties.

In 1902 Kano visited China on an official inspection tour of educational institutions. The Ch'ing Dynasty was crumbling and conditions in China were hardly ideal. Upon his return, Kano expanded the academy for Chinese exchange students that he had founded a few years earlier, in hopes that the students could get a "breath of fresh air" and then return to assist in the modernization of their homeland. Although it was not a requirement, several Chinese students took up judo at the Kodokan during their stay in Tokyo.

Overseas visitors were becoming a common sight at the Kodokan, and in 1903 an American industrialist named Samuel Hill invited Yoshiaki Yamashita (1875–1935) to teach his son Kodokan Judo in the United States. Yamashita had achieved fame at the Kodokan as the first trainee to attempt 10,000 contests in a single year (he fell a little short at 9,617). Yamashita accepted Hill's offer, but unfortunately Hill had not consulted sufficiently with his wife, and upon Yamashita's arrival in the United States the deal fell through owing to Mrs. Hill adamant opposition—"Judo is violent and rude."

●

●

Family man Kano with his wife and six children in 1902. The couple had two more children, a girl and a boy, the latter born when Kano was fifty-two years old.

Hill lined up other teaching jobs for Yamashita, however, and succeed in arranging a meeting with President Roosevelt at the White House. After reading *Bushido: The Soul of Japan* by Inazo Nitobe (1862–1933) Roosevelt developed a keen interest in Japanese martial arts. President Roosevelt wanted a demonstration of Kodokan Judo, and as a result the 5'4", 150-pound Yamashita faced off against an American wrestler nearly twice his size. Yamashita threw the wrestler repeatedly and finally pinned him. Impressed, Roosevelt helped him obtain a position teaching judo at the U.S. Naval Academy for the sum of $5,000, a princely salary for the times. Yamashita's charming wife, accomplished in judo herself, taught high society ladies. The couple had a fulfilling two-year stay in the United States.

Much less successful was the visit of Jojiro Tomita and Mitsuyo Maeda (1880–1941) to the White House in 1904, the following year. President Roosevelt wanted a judo instructor to stay in the capital since Yamashita was teaching elsewhere. Kano recommended Tomita, his senior disciple. Tomita was a dignified, cultured man with some knowledge of English, but his judo was not on a par with that of Saigo, Yokoyama, or Yamashita. Furthermore, some years back he had seriously injured his shoulder. Kano was aware of Tomita's limitations, as can be seen from the fact that he assigned Maeda, who at the time was considered the strongest young judo man at the Kodokan, to accompany him. Evidently, the plan was to have Maeda engage in the matches while Tomita explained the theory of Kodokan Judo. This plan worked well enough during a

•

•

demonstration at West Point, where Maeda countered the attacks of first a football player and then a boxer. At a White House reception, however, things did not go so well. After a formal demonstration of Kodokan Judo by Tomita and Maeda, an American football player in the audience issued an impromptu challenge. This time Tomita took the floor instead of Maeda, with unfortunate results: he failed with a throw and was helplessly pinned beneath the football player's bulk. President Roosevelt diplomatically called off any further matches, adding that Tomita was obviously under the weather, and the entire party was escorted into the White House for dinner.

Tomita made his way back to Japan not long after this incident, but Maeda, abashed by Tomita's poor showing and frantic to reassert the superiority of Kodokan Judo, stayed on. He persuaded some Japanese businessmen to stake him $1,000 in prize money and embarked on a long career of challenging all comers throughout North and South America. The 5'5", 154-pound Maeda was said to have engaged in 1,000 challenge matches, never once losing a judo-style competition and only once or twice suffering defeats as a professional wrestler. In Brazil, where he eventually settled, he was feted as Conte Comte ("Count Combat") and his savage system of fighting, now called "Gracie Jujutsu," is employed by certain fighters in present-day "no-holds-barred" professional matches.

Around the time that Maeda was touring as a fighter, an American named Ed Santeru was doing much the same. ("Santeru" is his last name as reproduced in Japanese *katakana*; I was unable to ascertain the English

●

●

spelling.) In addition to being a first-rate Western-style wrestler, Santeru quickly picked up techniques from his contests with jujutsu and Kodokan Judo men. (Besides the Kodokan Judo representatives mentioned above, there were Japanese jujutsu men from other schools roaming the United States as early as 1880.) Given Santeru's combat experience, Japanese martial artists lost the element of surprise, and soon Santeru was regularly defeating or at least drawing with Kodokan Judo men. It is said that he even stormed the Japanese headquarters itself, later declaring himself the "Judo World Champion." His last recorded match was held in Los Angeles in 1924 against a Kodokan Judo man named Ota. The three round match ended in a draw.

Kano deplored such free-for-all challenge matches right from the start—he banished his favorite and most promising disciple, Saigo, for violating that rule—and several times he issued bans against the practice, denouncing it as "contrary to the spirit of Kodokan Judo." Never at any time in Kodokan Judo under Kano was victory in competition the be all and end all. Late in life, after observing a tournament, a terribly disappointed Kano gathered the participants together and scolded them: "You fought like young bulls locking horns; there was nothing refined or dignified about any of the techniques I witnessed today. I never taught anyone to do Kodokan Judo like that. If all you think about is winning through brute strength, that will be end of Kodokan Judo."

The futility of relying on technique alone was proven time and time again. In 1929, for example, the proud and confident Judo Club of Waseda University visited the United States and engaged in a challenge tournament against the Wrestling Club of Washington University. The first round was fought with Kodokan Judo rules; the Japanese side won 10–0. The second round was contested with the rules of Western-style wrestling. The American side captured every match, 10–0. The rules for the final round were to be decided by the flip of a coin. The Japanese side won the toss, but instead of securing an expected easy victory they ended up losing or drawing every match save one. While the Waseda University judo men remained confused and flustered by the style of their opponents, the Washington University wrestlers had learned what to expect and adjusted their techniques accordingly, beating the Japanese at their own game.

While all these challenge matches were taking place in the United States, Kodokan Judo was well on its way to establishing itself in Europe. Again, initial interest was typically piqued by news of a diminutive Japanese flipping a large European to the ground, but once the novelty wore off serious practice of Kodokan Judo began. Incidentally, the practice of judo became popular among British suffragettes, and in 1913 a group of judo women formed a group called "The Bodyguard" to protect women speakers from rowdy men.

During the Russo-Japanese war of 1904–1905, a number of senior Kodokan members died in battle, including General Hirose and Admiral Asano. Kano warned his countrymen against developing false confidence over Japan's heady victories over China and Russia. China, burdened with a hopelessly corrupt imperial court and in-effectual army, more or less defeated itself; Russia was unable to supply the distant Far Eastern front with suffi-cient men or materiel, and if the war had been waged closer to Moscow, the outcome would have been much different. "War is never a good thing," Kano wrote, "and continual fighting will eventually led to defeat."

In 1906 the Kodokan expanded again, this time to a new 207-mat dojo in Shimo-Tomisaka-cho. Around this time, the *judogi* (practice uniform) was standardized in the form we see today. (In the old days the pants were often quite short, and the jackets quilted in different patterns.) In 1908 the Japanese Diet passed a bill requiring all mid-dle school students to be instructed in either kendo or judo.

In 1909 Kano was selected as the first Japanese mem-ber of the International Olympic Committee. While Kano was an extremely conscientious member, and eventually arranged for the 1940 Olympics to be scheduled for Tokyo, he had a somewhat ambivalent attitude toward the inclusion of Kodokan Judo in those games. As mentioned above, Kano was deeply troubled by the increasing em-phasis on winning, and he was worried that judo in the Olympics would became an instrument of nationalism. He was in favor of international open tournaments, of course, but he did not want to see country pitted against country as a measure of racial superiority. (Judo was not included in the Olympics until 1964, long after Kano was dead, and it is safe to say that the judo displayed there has little in common with the original ideals of Kodokan Judo.)

Kano was a teaching and traveling dynamo during the

•
•

The urbane and stylish judo master in his mid-fifties. Kano may have visited more foreign countries than any other Japanese of his generation, and this dignified gentleman acted as his nation's *de facto* foreign minister for nearly forty years.

years from 1910 through 1920. He retired as principal of the Tokyo Higher Normal School at age sixty, and then set off on a long trip to Europe and the United States. The Kodokan was spared serious damage in the Great Kanto Earthquake of 1923, and Kano's travels and lectures continued unabated. He even delivered a talk on "The Necessity of English Education in Today's International Society." In 1926 a Woman's Division was formally inaugurated at the Kodokan. Kano had always actively encouraged women to practice judo—he used to remark, "If you really want to understand judo, watch the women train." Perhaps Kano's top woman disciple was Keiko Fukuda (b. 1914), granddaughter of his first teacher, Hachinosuke Fukuda, and author of the English-language book *Born for the Mat.*

In 1927 Kano had a chance to visit Okinawa, where he investigated Okinawan culture, including karate. There Kano witnessed a battle between a mongoose and a deadly poisonous adder. (Such battles were, and still are, staged for tourists.) As is usually the case, the mongoose killed the adder because, as Kano observed, the animal practiced judo: "It dodged the adder's strike and immediately counterattacked with perfect timing."

While in Okinawa Kano was asked how a judo man would handle himself against a wild animal. He replied, "The most dangerous animal we are likely to encounter on mainland Japan is a bear. Bears are ferocious when cornered, but they will shy away from loud noises or bright lights. The best kind of judo is to keep the bear at bay with proper precaution rather than attempt to con-

•

43

•

front it face to face."

In 1929 the Indian philosopher and Nobel Prize win-
ner Rabindranath Tagore (1861–1941) visited the Kodokan and asked Kano to send a judo instructor to teach at
the university he was building in Bombay. Judo, the gentle
way, took root among the Hindus of India and is still practiced avidly there today.

The last twenty-five years of Kano's life were spent in
almost constant travel at home and abroad. Altogether he
made thirteen trips overseas in his lifetime, visiting the
four corners of the world. Despite the continuous series of
arduous trips, Kano never complained of travel fatigue; he
even disliked to hear the phrase *otsukare-sama deshita*
("You must be tired!"), dismissing any such greeting prof-
fered him upon returning from a journey.

Kano loved life. He relished the fine cooking and good
drink of East and West (but hated smoking—he would
refuse to attend banquets at which smoking was permitted.) An enthusiastic calligrapher and *shakuhachi* player,
Kano patronized traditional Japanese arts, especially classical music and dance. He enjoyed serious discussions on
national and international affairs, and often the informal
meetings in his office at the Kodokan lasted well past
midnight.

Given his peripatetic life-style, it is not surprising that
Kano died on a journey. In 1938 Kano attended an
Olympic Committee meeting in Cairo, and arranged for
the 1940 Olympics to be held in Tokyo. (They were ulti-
mately canceled owing to the outbreak of World War II.)
European delegates wanted to hold the games in August,

Kano (right) demonstrating a solid Kodokan Judo stance with Kyuzo Mifune (1883–1965), perhaps the greatest of Kano's many great students. Mifune's judo specialty was *kuki-nage*, "air throw." Those throws were so perfectly timed and dynamically executed that his opponents found nothing to resist—the technique was "empty." Judo on this level is essentially the same as aikido, which Kano called, after witnessing Morihei Ueshiba demonstrate, the "ideal budo."

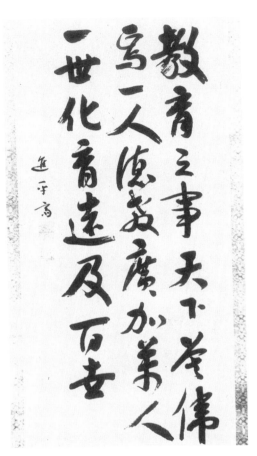

教育之事天下莫偉
焉一人徳教廣加萬人
一世化育遠及百世

Calligraphy by Jigoro Kano: "Nothing under heaven is more important than education: The teaching of one virtuous person can influence many; that which has been learned well by one generation can be passed on to a hundred." The brushstrokes reflect Kano's character: bold, confident, and perfectly balanced.

•

•

but Kano suggested September instead: "The weather in Japan in August is very hot and humid; Japanese competitors, who are accustomed to such muggy conditions, would have a decided advantage over athletes from other countries." On the return trip to Tokyo aboard the Hikawa-maru, Kano fell ill and died peacefully on May 4, 1938, aged seventy-eight.

Kano's life and teaching can be best summed up by the words he wrote when he established Kodokan Judo: "The teaching of one virtuous person can influence many; that which has been learned well by one generation can be passed on to a hundred."

Gichin Funakoshi

(1868–1957)

WHILE JIGORO KANO AND MORIHEI Ueshiba are recognized as the respective "founders" of Kodokan Judo and aikido, Gichin Funakoshi is perceived as being the "father" of modern karate, a representative of, and role model for, that style of budo rather than its actual inventor. Funakoshi also emerged from a milieu quite different from that which nutured Kano and Ueshiba. In order to understand Funakoshi's position as one of the three budo masters, we must first consider the distinctive culture of Okinawa.

The principal island of the Ryukyu chain, Okinawa lies 300 miles south of the edge of mainland Japan, and it is 1,000 miles distant from Tokyo. Okinawa is a small island, only about forty-five square miles in area, with a sub-tropical climate that would qualify as benign were it not for the constant threat of typhoons—as many as forty-five can occur in the vicinity in a single year, and direct hits are both frequent and frightening. The soil is rocky, the forest cover thin, and outside of the typhoon season of March through September fresh water was (and is) often in short supply. In the seventeenth century sugar cane and sweet potatoes became the principal crops. Little else flourished on the island, and the Okinawans depended greatly on the sea for their survival, which supplied them with fish and brought trading ships to their shores. The population of Okinawa at the beginning of the twentieth century was around 120,000.

Ancient Okinawan culture had a definite matriarchal cast to it. Although principalities were ostensibly ruled jointly by a king and a high priestess, troops were sent into battle in the name of the high priestess, not the king (for goddesses were regarded as the true protectors of human beings), and the priestess also settled legal disputes. Just as the high priestess officiated at the major rites of the ruling court, the senior female member of the household conducted the important family rituals. The standing of women on Okinawa had been somewhat eroded by the introduction of Confucianism and Buddhism in the fifteenth and sixteenth centuries—in Okinawan theater Buddhist priests are always portrayed as great villains—but women there in general remained on a much more equal footing with men than was the case for the women of China and Japan.

The constantly warring Three Kingdoms of Northern, Central, and Southern Okinawa were unified in 1429 under Sho Hashi, founder of the Sho Dynasty. During the reign of Sho Shin (1477–1526), a Confucian state was established and a ban on the private ownership of weapons was imposed on the populace. Thanks to lucrative trading with China, Japan, and the rest of Southeast Asia, the Kingdom of Ryukyu flourished until it was invaded in 1609 by the pugnacious samurai of Satsuma, a fief in Kyushu, the southernmost island of mainland Japan. The Satsuma fief was the most warlike in Japan, with a samurai to commoner ratio of one-to-three (the national average was one-to-seventeen).

Although the Kingdom of Ryukyu retained its nominal independence, the tiny nation was slowly bled dry by the dual burdens of continued tribute payments to the Chinese court and unequal trade agreements with the overlords of Satsuma. While they may have suffered materially, the Okinawans maintained their rich spiritual culture centered on music, poetry, dance, and the general celebration of life. Satsuma overlords reinforced the ban on the private ownership of weapons and later even prohibited the importation of weapons by the government for purposes of self-defense. Word of the "Peaceful Kingdom" of Ryukyu reached Napoleon in France, who marveled that any country could maintain peace and order without recourse to weapons. Many visitors, past and present, have similarly commented on the "hospitality, kindness, and aversion to violence and crime" of the Okinawans.

They may have been without weapons, but the Okinawans were certainly neither weak nor defenseless. The legend of Okinawan peasants creating karate to defend themselves against the flagrant attacks of Satsuma samurai bullies does not seem to have much basis in fact. The ban against weapons had already been in effect for over a

•

•

hundred years prior to the Satsuma invasion. Yet as a practical matter, it is true that unarmed constables needed to rely on some means to guard the populace and subdue troublemakers, while ordinary citizens required a form of self-defense against thugs and ruffians, who exist in even the most peaceful societies.

In that Okinawa had been in close contact with China for centuries, it is not surprising that "Chinese Hand"—the original meaning of "karate"—referred to the many martial art forms based on Chinese models that were practiced on the island. Okinawans learned various forms of boxing during their trading trips to China, and immigrant Chinese *kempo* (*ch'uan fu*) masters taught on the island itself. There is evidence that some techniques were imported from the empty-handed fighting systems of Indochina as well. Much of this boxing never went beyond the level of street-fighting, a popular diversion in raucous Okinawan ports.

In addition to imported Chinese boxing, more indigenous martial art forms were apparently formulated over the centuries by the upper-classes of Okinawa. These native systems were referred to as *okinawa-te*, "Okinawan Hand." Deprived of conventional armaments, the Okinawans devised methods to turn everyday implements such as a staff or sickle into lethal weapons. The suspicious Satsuma overlords ordered many of those tools to be locked up in government warehouses at night, requiring farmers and fishermen to check them out again each morning. There was also a type of competitive wrestling called *tegumi*, somewhat akin to sumo, which was openly engaged in by men and boys of all ages.

With the exception of *tegumi*, the Okinawan martial arts were practiced in strict secrecy to avoid the scrutiny of both the Satsuma overlords and rival schools. Martial techniques were considered family heirlooms, and guarded zealously from generation to generation. (Many karate moves were cleverly incorporated into Okinawan folk dance, however, and even today some schools include folk dancing as part of the training curriculum.) Martial arts in Okinawa never enjoyed the popular support accorded the practice of budo on mainland Japan, and on the island there never existed a comparable class of well-armed professional warriors such as the samurai. There were in fact no dojo in Okinawa in the old days—karate was practiced at night behind garden walls, in the deep forest, along deserted beaches. Nor were there uniform training outfits—the Okinawan karate practitioners usually wore next to nothing. Also in contrast to Japan, where techniques were carefully catalogued on scrolls and transmission lineages clearly delineated, on Okinawa almost nothing was written down, no records kept, making it virtually impossible to draw any concrete conclusions about the history of the martial arts there.

From this we can see that both the material and the martial culture into which Gichin Funakoshi was born differed significantly from that experienced by Jigoro Kano and Morihei Ueshiba on mainland Japan.

Gichin Funakoshi was born in the Okinawan royal capital of Shuri, probably in November of 1868. His official birth year is recorded as 1870, but in his autobiography

•

•

Funakoshi claimed that this was a later alteration made in order to allow him to sit for an examination only open to those born in 1870 or thereafter. The dedication stone on Funakoshi's gravest gives the 1870 date, however, and it appears that Funakoshi indiscriminately used both birth dates throughout his life—that is, he did not really know in what year he was born.

Funakoshi's family was of the *shizoku* (gentry) class. (The family name was originally read as "Tominakoshi.") His grandfather was a renowned Confucian scholar who once tutored the royal family. He was given a large pension by the government upon retirement, but his profligate son, Gisu, Funakoshi's father, squandered the family fortune on potent *awamori* liquor and gambling. Born two months premature and not expected to live much beyond infancy, Funakoshi was sent to be cared for by his doting grandparents. He surprised everyone by growing up to be a normal, healthy boy, albeit somewhat on the puny side. His grandfather taught him the Chinese classics from an early age, and the boy proved to be a keen and talented student.

Funakoshi appeared on the scene just as the old order was being rudely confronted by the new, and he was caught squarely in the middle. The Meiji reforms of mainland Japan reached distant Okinawa after some delay (the King of Okinawa was not formally deposed until 1879), but once the new laws were promulgated, battle lines were drawn between the "Enlightenment Party" and the "Obstinate Party." Okinawan nobles had no qualms about being denied the privilege of wearing two swords as were the samurai on mainland Japan (a privilege they never had enjoyed at any rate), but they were fanatically attached to their kimono-style clothing and, especially, their topknots. Those topknots (which were more like the type worn in China than mainland Japan) were a sign of status and good breeding to Okinawan nobles, and loss of that symbol meant the end of their world (which was exactly what the Meiji reformers had in mind.)

As a teenager, Funakoshi himself had no strong feelings about the issue, but this was not true of his family, who were die-hard supporters of the Obstinate Party. Family feeling was so strong, in fact, that Funakoshi was forced to give up the place he had won for himself at the Tokyo Medical College because the school would not enroll anyone wearing a topknot. When he accepted a teaching position in Okinawa in 1888 on the condition that he remove his topknot, his furious and heart-broken parents nearly disowned him. However, "the die was cast," as Funakoshi wrote. Both for himself and for Okinawa the old order was gone forever.

Funakoshi spent the next thirty years in and around Shuri and Naha (the new Okinawan capital), working as a teacher and training in karate. He states in his autobiography that he was introduced to karate when he was about eleven years old by a classmate, the son of the master Yasutsune Azato. However, other sources maintain that Funakoshi did not begin training until he was around twenty, and that his first teacher was Taitei Kinjo (1837–1917), nicknamed the "Iron Fist" for his ability to stop an ox dead in its tracks with a single blow. Kinjo was apparently a rough, ill-tempered fellow, and it was only a matter of months before Funakoshi left. He then went to board with Azato, where his training began in earnest under a teacher he respected and loved.

Even though Azato (1828–1906) came from a high-ranking noble family, he was a staunch supporter of the Enlightenment Party, among the first of the gentry to divest himself of his topknot. Tall and broad-shouldered, Azato was an accomplished scholar as well as a master of many martial arts—karate, kendo, archery, and horsemanship. Since karate, in keeping with tradition and the Meiji government's ban on Okinawan fighting arts (as a potential threat to the fledgling regime), was still not openly practiced, the training sessions took place at night in Azato's garden. Azato advised Funakoshi, "Turn your hands and feet into swords," and he mercilessly drilled him in *kata*. In judo, *kata* are patterned forms usually practiced with a partner, while in karate, *kata* are generally practiced individually and consist of sequences that include basic and advanced punches, kicks, blocks, and evasive movements. Master Azato was not easily impressed, and it would often be months before Funakoshi was allowed to move on to another *kata*.

After training, Azato would often give Funakoshi pointers on the psychological dimensions of karate. He maintained that proper deportment and dignified manners were just as important as technique. Funakoshi was amazed by Azato's detailed and accurate knowledge of the other martial art teachers on Okinawa—their names, where they lived, their strengths and weaknesses. "The secret of victory," Azato told Funakoshi, "is to know both yourself and your opponent through careful preparation and close observation. That way you will never be caught off guard." Azato applied this approach to world affairs as well, astutely predicting a war between Russia and Japan long before it actually occurred.

Funakoshi's other main teacher was Azato's comrade Yasutsune Itosu (1831–1916), another nobleman who had been an important official in the old government. He had retired from government service in 1885 and was teaching karate to a few selected students at his home. Itosu was only of average height, but he had a barrel chest, a body like granite, and extraordinary arm strength. Even using both hands, Azato was unable to defeat Itosu in arm-wrestling, and Itosu could crush a thick stalk of bamboo with his viselike grip. It is said that Itosu would pay a visit to the Imperial Tombs every day, and on his way to and fro he would practice his punches against the stone walls lining the road. He could also punch through thick boards, a talent he once put to good use when he found himself locked out of friend's party—he punched a hole in the heavy gate, unlatched the lock, and let himself him. Famed for his balanced temper even when faced with an unprovoked attack, he would let the blows bounce harmlessly off his body before calmly bringing the attacker to his knees by merely seizing his wrist. Under Itosu's direction, Funakoshi spent ten years mastering three basic *kata*.

Funakoshi also studied briefly with Azato's and Itosu's principal mentor, Sokon Matsumura (1809–1901), the "Miyamoto Musashi of Okinawa." Over six feet tall and possessed of a mesmerizing gaze, Matsumura served as a court instructor and chief bodyguard for a succession of Okinawan kings. As a government envoy, he honed his skill in Chinese boxing in Fuchu Province and learned Jigen Ryu swordsmanship in Satsuma. Matsumura was furthermore a first-rate scholar and calligrapher. His wife, Tsuru, was as accomplished as he was, and they had had an unusual courtship. A tomboy in the traditional Okinawan fashion, Tsuru defeated every man she faced in arm-wrestling, weight lifting, or karate. Matsumura thought she would be just the girl for him, but Tsuru refused to wooed by anyone who could not defeat her. When Matsumura took up the challenge, Tsuru landed a clean strike that he was unable to counter. The match was close enough to be interesting, however, so she gave him another chance, and this time the blows were simultaneous. A draw was good enough for Tsuru, and so she and Matsumura were married.

(A similar tale is told of the Edo beauty Rui Sasaki. Daughter of a Tokugawa retainer, Rui was a master of jujutsu and swordsmanship, and her proud father told her, "Never forget you are as good as any man." He died at an early age, alas, and it was up to Rui to continue the family line. She opened a dojo in Edo and took on all comers, until one day she met her match. That was the man she married, he adopting the family name.)

While certain modern karate men have achieved notoriety by fighting bulls, this practice has a long history in Okinawa, as we have already seen. The king of Okinawa once challenged Matsumura to try his luck against the

fiercest fighting bull in the land. (In Okinawan bullfight-
ing, where two bulls that are pitted against one another,
the animals are bred for absolute meanness.) Matsumura
accepted, and that very evening and every evening thereafter for a week, wearing the same clothes, the clever
karate master sneaked into the bull's pen and whacked it
over the head a few times with a heavy rod. On the day of
the event a large crowd gathered to watch—Warrior Matsumura versus Killer Bull. The bull, released from its pen,
charged furiously towards the center of the ring. There it
abruptly pulled up, seeing its opponent—Matsumura in
familiar clothing, holding a heavy rod. Immediately the
terrified beast turned tail. The crowd was delighted, hail-
ing Matsumura as the "Master who can defeat a raging
bull just with his gaze."

Funakoshi also trained with other teachers on Okinawa, the most prominent being Kanryo Higaonna (1853–
1917). Higaonna (also pronounced Toonno) had spent
much of his youth mastering boxing in China. From there
he brought back various types of weights, punching bags,
iron clogs, and the like, which he introduced into Okinawan karate training. Higaonna told his students, "In
karate training, as well as in life, when something blocks
your path, step aside and move around it." Funakoshi
also seems to have familiarized himself with Okinawan
weapons, especially the *bo* (six-foot staff), which he may
have learned from his father, an acknowledged master of
the weapon.

In addition to training under many of the outstanding
masters of Okinawa, Funakoshi was constantly forging his

body. Hour upon hour he spent hardening his fists and elbows against the *makiwara*, the karate punching board.
When a typhoon blew up, Funakoshi would grab a thick
straw mat, climb to the roof of his house, assume the
karate "horse-stance," holding the straw mat in front of his
body as protection against flying objects, and confront the
storm in direct combat. He walked ten to fifteen miles a
day, commuting to school during the day and karate training at night; he lifted heavy weights and wore cast iron
scandals; he arm-wrestled; he joined tug-of-war teams.
(One thing he did not do was swim, never learning how in
spite of living on a semitropical island.)

As mentioned above, Okinawan women were noted for
their strength and determination. Funakoshi's wife was no
exception. The Funakoshi's family of ten—four children
(three sons and one daughter), his parents and grandparents—were not well off, and Mrs. Funakoshi had to dye
cloth and raise vegetables to help make ends meet. In spite
of her heavy daily schedule she started practicing karate
together with her husband at night, and soon she was
nearly as skillful as he was. Funakoshi usually had a few
students training with him, and when he was absent Mrs.
Funakoshi would lead the sessions.

During these years in Okinawa, Funakoshi had many
opportunities to apply karate in practical situations. Dealing with street toughs, rambunctious drunks, and petty
criminals did not present a problem for the karate master.
Once, for example, he admonished a ruffian who was be-
having badly at a banquet. The ruffian urinated on Funakoshi to provoke a fight. Funakoshi let him attack, but

the ruffian failed to land a single blow. Eventually he collapsed to the ground in exhaustion, his fury dissipated. Funakoshi had not thrown a single punch, letting the rowdy fellow defeat himself.

Funakoshi's most harrowing encounter on Okinawa was when he and his eldest son crossed paths with one of the huge, deadly vipers that thrive on the island. Funakoshi remained calm, not giving the snake a chance to strike, and he and his child escaped unscathed.

Funakoshi's greatest karate challenges came in mediating disputes between various clashing parties. He was frequently called upon to resolve problems between teachers and students in the local school system, and once he was asked by the police to mediate a long-standing dispute between two hamlets in the Kokuryo District of northern Okinawa. The contending parties squared off on neutral ground with Funakoshi in the middle. The atmosphere was tense, and violence could have erupted at any moment, but Funakoshi kept his head, defused the situation, and came up with an acceptable solution after two days of arduous, non-stop negotiation. He later wrote that it was his karate training that gave him the stamina and the presence of mind to overcome the obstacles he faced during this incident. Similarly, Mrs. Funakoshi was frequently requested to mediate disputes that broke out in her family's neighborhood.

During these years the practice of karate in Okinawa gradually came out into the open. Around 1892 Itosu and a few of his students gave a demonstration for Shintaro Ogawa, a visiting commissioner of education from mainland Japan, who then recommended that karate be taught at the First Public High School of Okinawa and the local Officers Candidate School. In 1901 (or perhaps 1902) Funakoshi himself gave a demonstration for Ogawa, and this led to karate being included in the physical education curriculum of Okinawan schools. Starting around 1906, public demonstrations of karate became common in Okinawa, with Funakoshi and some other leading practitioners cooperating to spread the art on the island.

Okinawan karate also caught the attention of mainland military officials. The first three successful officer candidates from Okinawa were students of Itosu, and the examining physicians made special note of their splendid physiques and excellent condition. One of the recruits, Kentsu Yabu (who will be mentioned again later) became a hero of the Sino-Japanese War, successfully defending his company's position even though outnumbered ten to one. In 1912 navy personnel were dispatched from the Imperial Fleet to learn karate in Okinawa.

In 1917 Funakoshi was invited to give a demonstration of Okinawan karate in the Butoku-den, the grand martial art hall in Kyoto. This is thought to be the first officially sponsored demonstration of karate outside of Okinawa. (There had been practitioners of Okinawan karate among the immigrants to mainland Japan—and Hawaii and the United States as well—from early in the Meiji period, but it seems that there had never been any previous formal presentations.)

Loath to accept a post at a distant school district and keen to devote himself to the promotion of karate, Funakoshi gave up his position as a teacher early in 1921. (It is said that during his entire thirty-year tenure, Funakoshi never once missed a class because of illness; he attributed his good health to a steady diet of karate.) In May of that year Crown Prince Hirohito, returning from a trip to Europe, stopped in Okinawa and witnessed a special demonstration of karate by Funakoshi's group, performed in the Great Hall of Shuri Castle. The Crown Prince loved it, and he later recalled that the three best things he had seen in Okinawa during his visit there were the beautiful scenery, the fantastic Magic Fountain Dragon Drain of Shuri Castle, and karate.

After his retirement from the Okinawan school system, Funakoshi busied himself forming several associations to promote Okinawan culture in general and karate in particular. In May of 1922, the Japanese Ministry of Education was to sponsor a National Athletic Exhibition in Tokyo which would include budo demonstrations. An invitation to the event was sent to the Okinawan Educational Affairs Office. This would be a crucial test for Okinawan karate on the mainland, and after much discussion it was decided to send Funakoshi as the Okinawan representative, although not necessarily as the most technically skilled. He was, after all, a scholar, an educator, a good public speaker, and in his mature fifties. The Okinawan officials concluded that Funakoshi would be the ideal representative.

Funakoshi planned very carefully for the demonstration, which was to take place before the highest echelons of Japanese society. His thoroughly prepared lecture (illustrated with three long scrolls) and a dynamic demonstration were well received. Jigoro Kano was particularly impressed, and he asked Funakoshi to teach a few suitable *kata* at the Kodokan. In fact, Kano had corresponded with Funakoshi several years earlier about the possibility of coming to teach at the Kodokan, but at that time Funakoshi had declined—"I'm still in the process of learning karate myself" had been his reply.

This time Funakoshi accepted the invitation, though not without trepidation. Initially he was awed by the intensity of the training at the Kodokan and the number, physical size, and high quality of the trainees—there was nothing like it on Okinawa. Nevertheless, Funakoshi's teaching at the Kodokan went well. Kano adopted certain of the karate movements Funakoshi demonstrated into an advanced judo *kata*, and asked Funakoshi to head up a Kodokan "Karate Division." Funakoshi felt compelled to decline, fearing that karate would be swallowed up by the huge Kodokan Judo organization and never amount to anything more than an auxiliary art. Funakoshi was nevertheless eternally grateful for Kano's kind initial support, and after the judo master's death in 1938 Funakoshi would bow in the direction of Kano's office whenever he passed by the Kodokan on the streetcar or in an automobile.

Although Funakoshi had originally intended to return to Okinawa, after teaching at the Kodokan he decided to remain in Tokyo. A number of prominent Okinawans (including members of the regal Sho family, exiled to Tokyo after the abolishment of the Okinawan monarchy in 1879) urged him to stay on in the capital and introduce karate to a wider audience. Furthermore, Funakoshi's eldest son had already taken up residence there. After making the decision to settle in Tokyo, Funakoshi composed this poem:

> The superlative techniques of the South Seas,
> this karate!
> What a pity to see the true transmission
> threatened.
> Who will take the challenge to restore karate
> to its full glory?
> With a steadfast heart, facing the azure sky,
> I make that solemn pledge.

Funakoshi sent for his wife, but she was reluctant to leave home. As mentioned earlier, Okinawan women were responsible for the performance of ancestral rites, and there were other binding ties as well. Yet she supported her husband's decision to stay in Tokyo, sensing that he might accomplish something of great importance there.

Largely on his own in a strange city, Funakoshi was faced with his greatest challenge. Okinawa had been a vassal state for centuries, and Okinawan things and people were typically dismissed as being second-rate by mainland Japanese, especially by those living in the capital. Okinawans were "different"—they were darker in complexion, they spoke a rough dialect, they were hopelessly provincial. It would not be easy convincing mainland Japanese that an Okinawan art had any real value, especially one that they considered to be derivative of Chinese boxing. Japanese samurai society had always been weapon orientated, and unarmed arts were for the hoi polloi. Many

•

•

Okinawans were disdainful of what the mainlanders thought of them, but Funakoshi was more accommodating, hoping to introduce the best aspects of Okinawan culture into the larger culture of Japan.

This would prove to be a long, hard struggle. Funakoshi was able to move into the Meisei Juku, a dormitory set up for students from Okinawa in the Suidobata area of Tokyo. He secured a tiny room on the premises, which he kept spotlessly clean, but because there were few students to begin with, he was without a steady income. Obliged to work as combination janitor, groundskeeper, and night watchman at the dormitory, he was often mistaken for a servant by neighbors, prospective students, and newspaper reporters. He was forced to persuade the dormitory cook to take karate lessons in exchange for a break on his food bill, and eventually he had to pawn the few items of value that he owned.

Despite his straitened circumstances, Funakoshi was able to publish, with the help of some supporters, the first book on modern karate near the end of 1922. Entitled simply *Ryukyu Kempo-Karate*, "Ryukyu Chinese-Hand Fist Techniques," it was illustrated with line drawings of the *kata*, and the book began with a number of testimonials from prominent Japanese on the virtues of the art (even though it was of Okinawan origin).

On September 1, 1923, just as Funakoshi had build up a small core of ten or so dedicated students, the Great Kanto Earthquake struck, killing over 100,000 people and destroying much of Tokyo. The Meisei Dormitory was damaged, some of Funakoshi's students were killed or seriously injured, and training, of course, came to a stop. Following the disaster, Funakoshi supported himself by working at a bank making piece-work stencils. While the Meisei dormitory was being repaired, Hakudo Nakayama (1874–1958), perhaps the top kendo master of the day, generously offered to let Funakoshi use his dojo during free hours. Even after the Meisei Dormitory was ready for use, Funakoshi continued to use the Nakayama Dojo. Eventually he rented a house in a nearby neighborhood, where he lived with his third son, Gigo, who had joined him in 1924.

Funakoshi gradually attracted more students, and karate clubs began to form at various universities. Keio was the first university to establish a club (in 1924), and was quickly followed by Takushoku, and then Waseda and Hosei. Karate clubs were soon functioning at most other major universities, and Funakoshi began teaching at a few military academies as well. Several gigantic sumo champions also sought instruction (although punching and kicking were not allowed in sumo, open-hand attacks were, and the wrestlers wanted to learn how to make more effective thrusts), which pleased the diminutive Funakoshi immensely.

Short even for a Japanese of that time, Funakoshi was rather self-conscious about his height. Whenever he went out in public, he wore high, single-toothed wooden sandals. "Not to increase my height," Funakoshi maintained, "but to improve my balance." His students noticed, however, that whenever they visited the master in his room, he was always sitting on two or three thick cushions. He was

Funakoshi leading a group of university students in *kata* training. Funakoshi's Shotokan style of karate employed fifteen basic *kata* to develop correct movements, stamina, sharp reflexes, firm muscles, and flexibility.

also quite fastidious about his general appearance, usually grooming himself for an hour or more each morning.

Funakoshi and his students participated in two other important budo demonstrations organized by the government during the decade, one in 1924 and the other in 1928, the latter coordinated by the Imperial Household Agency. A revised version of Funakoshi's textbook was published in 1926 with a new title: *Renten Goshin Karate Jutsu*, "Training and Self-Defense Karate Arts." Karate was on its way to assuming an central place in contemporary budo culture.

Around 1924 Funakoshi adopted a ranking system similar to that of the Kodokan, with practitioners of *dan* rank wearing black belts. His trainees tied their belts in the front, but for some reason Funakoshi wore his own belt tied to the side, which was more in the Chinese style. Funakoshi opted for a lighter-weight training uniform than

•

•

used in judo, to permit more freedom of movement for punches and kicks.

While Funakoshi deserves to be honored as the "father" of modern karate because of his promotion of the art in the capital of Tokyo and the wide dissemination of his excellent textbooks, there were a number of other karate pioneers from Okinawa who played significant roles in the expansion of karate both on the Japanese mainland and abroad.

Chokki Motobu (1871–1944) arrived in Osaka in 1921 in search of employment, the year before Funakoshi settled in Tokyo. Like Funakoshi, Motobu had studied under Itosu for a while, but most of his karate was learned on the street. Motobu was a brawler, and his aggressive style of karate centered on actual combat—he knew few *kata* and only gave instruction in one. He was seriously interested in classical jujutsu, which is another reason he came to Osaka. The first time he engaged in a trial match with a jujutsu teacher, he knocked out his opponent without working up a sweat. Motobu further made a name for himself in Osaka by decking a foreign heavyweight boxer with a single blow. (Motobu was over fifty at the time.)

Subsequently, Motobu opened dojo in both Osaka and Tokyo, and he instructed at different universities (relying on an interpreter to translate his Okinawan dialect into standard Japanese). In 1926 he published a book on karate called *Ryukyu Kempo Karate Jutsu: Kumite Hen*, "Ryukyu Chinese-Hand Fist Technique Arts: Sparring Edition," to distinguish it from Funakoshi's book, which focused on *kata*. Motobu was Funakoshi's diametric opposite in character and karate style, and the two men never seemed to be on good terms. Motobu is reported to have mellowed with age, however, and near the end of his life his vision of karate as a refined, spiritual art was probably much the same as that of Funakoshi's. Motobu returned to Okinawa just before the outbreak of World War II, and died in Naha in 1944.

Funakoshi was much closer to Chojun Miyagi (1888–1953) and Kenwa Mabuni (1889–1952). Miyagi, who had been a member of the group that demonstrated before Crown Prince Hirohito in 1921, was primarily a student of Kanryo Higaonna, but as a businessman he also had many chances to visit China and was thus familiar with various schools of Chinese boxing. Miyagi also emphasized the connection between karate and Buddhist philosophy. During his visit to Okinawa in 1927, Jigoro Kano encouraged both Miyagi and Mabuni to teach karate on the mainland. (Miyagi later recalled that, regardless of the judo master's eminence, Kano was one of the most polite and considerate individuals that he had ever met, and he considered him a giant among men.) Both karate men followed Kano's advice. Miyagi first visited mainland Japan in 1928, making many trips thereafter, and in 1934 he visited Hawaii for eight months on a highly acclaimed instruction tour. (In 1932 Motobu was refused entry into Hawaii by immigration authorities, no doubt owing to his reputation as a street fighter, and was sent straight back to Japan.) Miyagi is credited with being the founder of the Goju ("Hard-Soft") style of karate. He died in Naha of a cerebral hemorrhage in 1953.

Mabuni, who was originally an Okinawan policeman, had trained under Higaonna and Itosu. He joined Funakoshi in Tokyo in 1928, but the next year he moved to Osaka, likely in deference to Funakoshi's seniority—there were not yet enough students in Tokyo to support two karate teachers. Like Funakoshi, Mabuni was poverty-stricken his first years on the mainland, but in 1934 managed to open up a small dojo and thereafter publish a variety of pamphlets on his style of karate, the Shito Ryu. The name indicates a blending of the Higaonna and Itosu styles of karate. Mabuni stressed the careful study and execution of a wide selection of *kata*—he himself was believed to have had seventy or eighty at his command, more than any other master of the time. Mabuni settled permanently in Osaka and died there in 1952.

Another Okinawan immigrant to mainland Japan was Kanbun Uechi (1877–1942), founder of the Uechi Ryu, perhaps the largest and most influential karate school today in Okinawa. Uechi taught karate in Wakayama from 1925 to 1946. Kentsu Yabu (1866–1937), the heroic soldier mentioned previously, seems to have taught karate to Japanese immigrants in Los Angeles and Hawaii as early as 1920. He also spent four months instructing in Hawaii in 1927. (During the twenties and thirties, Japanese immigrants on the U.S. West Coast and in Hawaii were increasingly subject to unprovoked attacks by racists and thus understandably eager to learn judo and karate.)

One of Funakoshi's first students was Hironori Otsuka (1893–1982), who was already an accomplished jujutsu master of the Shindo Yoshin Ryu when he took up karate.

•

•

Otsuka, who also trained under Motobu and Mabuni and studied with Ueshiba, went on to establish the Wado Ryu, one of the major schools of karate. Masatatsu Oyama (1923–94), the colorful and controversial creator of knockout Kyokushinkai Karate, was also once a student of Funakoshi's. "Master Funakoshi straightened me out," Oyama said. "He showed me the true meaning of karate." In one way or another, Funakoshi had relationships with all of the principal karate pioneers.

Sometime during the late 1920s or early 1930s Funakoshi met Morihei Ueshiba. The two were most likely introduced by either Admiral Isamu Takeshita (1869–1949) or by Hakudo Nakayama. Funakoshi attended Ueshiba's special seminars and also visited his dojo from time to time to exchange views on the true nature of budo.

In 1935 Funakoshi published a new book. The title itself announced significant changes: *Karate-Do Kyohan*, "The Way of Karate: Master Text." Karate was no longer a mere art, it was a "Way," and Funakoshi's spelling of *karate* no longer meant "Chinese hand," but rather "empty hand." Substitution of the character *kara*, "empty," for *kara*, "Chinese," had been under discussion for some years among Okinawan instructors. As far back as 1905 a karate man named Chomo Hanashiro (1869–1945) had suggested the change, and the Keio University Karate Club actually made the substitution in 1929. Funakoshi's declaration helped make the change permanent. Undoubtedly Japanese nationalism also had something to do with the switch of characters, but Funakoshi preferred to inter-

Karate master Gichin Funakoshi in his mid-sixties. Sickly as a child, Funakoshi was extraordinarily healthy as an adult, thanks (he often reminded his students) to the practice of karate—"the best medicine there is."

pret this new version of "karate" as signifying "empty-handed technique," "empty of selfish and evil thoughts," "empty like the hollow bamboo yet straight, pliant, and unbreakable," and "empty of self-being, synonymous with the truth of the universe." Funakoshi also replaced the old pronunciations of the *kata* names, which were mostly in a bastardized Chinese, with more elegant, standard Japanese readings.

By 1936 sufficient funds had been collected to open a true karate dojo. Funakoshi's students named it "Shotokan" in honor of their teacher—*Shoto*, "Pine-Waves," being his penname. Thereafter Funakoshi's style of karate was typically referred to as "Shotokan Ryu," although he himself discouraged such designations, believing that all karate was "one" and should remain free of sectarian distinctions. Practically speaking, however, karate differed greatly in technique and approach from master to master, and it was natural that various styles should be recognized as forming separate "streams" (the original meaning of *ryu*). The Shotokan style became one such stream. Ironically, while the Shotokan Ryu was the driving force behind the introduction of Okinawan karate to the world, it never became well established on the island itself.

After the Shotokan opened, Funakoshi's third son, Gigo (1907–45), became his chief assistant. By all accounts, Gigo (a few inches taller than his father and about fifteen pounds heavier) was technically gifted and extraordinarily powerful—he constantly shattered *makiwara* punching boards with his blows. Despite such strength, however, Gigo was not a well man. Having contracted

•

76

•

tuberculosis as a small child in Okinawa, he frequently had to take a break during training to cough up blood.

At the Shotokan, Funakoshi Senior was known as the "Old Master," and Funakoshi Junior, the "Young Master." Those titles hinted at the clash between generations. When students would crack floorboards with their stomp kicks, Funakoshi Junior would yell out in praise, "Good! Good!" But if Funakoshi Senior was leading the class, he would scold, "What is the matter with you? That is too much force, too much force!" For the father, the heart of karate was *kata* training, practical self-defence, and character development: "Technique does not make the man; the man makes the technique!" To the less idealistic son, karate needed to formulate a competitive element, similar to that of kendo and judo, in order to attract and hold the interest of young people. Competition had already begun among college karate clubs, and Gigo believed that the Shotokan should follow suit. The issue was never settled between the old and young masters, as Gigo died prematurely, but there was a clear difference between students trained by Funakoshi Senior and Junior.

In Funakoshi Senior's classes, the emphasis was on *kata* training in order to develop fully all of the muscles and reflexes. Sparring practice was based on the premise that a single blow must decide all (*ikken hisatsu*); an attack was to be immediately countered, ideally stopped in its tracks by grabbing the opponent's sleeve. Some throws and pins were utilized. Funakoshi Senior permitted some free-sparring but only after the basics of karate had been thoroughly understood. In Funakoshi Junior's classes, on the other hand, postures were more fluid and upright for speed of attack, and full extension kicks were frequently employed—elements that were valuable in free-style competition for scoring points.

No matter who was leading the sessions, however, the training at the Shotokan was grueling. Both Funakoshis were demons on the *makiwara*, striking it hundreds and hundreds of times a day, and they made their students do the same. *Kata* were practiced fifty or sixty times in succession. Only one in ten trainees at the Shotokan could keep up the pace for more than a few months. Students

Funakoshi punching away at the *makiwara*. Funakoshi was a demon for training, and he forged his fists and elbows against the *makiwara* hundreds of times a day, right to the end of his long life of nearly ninety years. Funakoshi was small in stature, but his hip and arm power were remarkable.

who did last, though, received special individual instruction at the Funakoshi home at night. A student would go through a *kata*, with both father and son offering pointers. This traditional manner of karate instruction was the same as it had been in Okinawa.

As Japan headed into World War II, training at the Shotokan took on a do-or-die intensity. A hand-to-hand fight to the death was a real possibility for young men soon to be sent to the front. As the war moved closer to home, women were sent to the Shotokan to receive instruction in stave and wooden-sword fighting. Deluded military leaders believed that malnourished women could somehow be taught to fight off American invaders, armed to the teeth, in the streets of Tokyo. The atmosphere was grim, and a sense of impending doom pervaded the country.

Nineteen forty-five was the worst year of Funakoshi's life. The Shotokan, "the crowning achievement" of his career, was reduced to ashes during the Tokyo air raids; Okinawa was leveled during the invasion by U.S. forces, with 60,000 civilians killed and ninety percent of the survivors left homeless, a scale of destruction that rivalled that of Hiroshima and Nagasaki; Japan surrendered in ignominious defeat in August, leaving the nation in ruins; and Funakoshi's son Gigo died of leukemia. Miraculously, his wife had been able to escape the devastation on Okinawa and make it to Oita, Kyushu, where Funakoshi joined her. Food scarce, they lived in dire poverty (like everyone else), and in 1947 Mrs. Funakoshi died of asthma.

Bereft of his beloved wife and son Gigo, Funakoshi

sadly returned to Tokyo to live with his son Yoshihide.

Funakoshi had a complex relationship with his first son. In his youth, Yoshihide had been an enthusiastic karate trainee and practiced under Itosu together with his father, but after his move to Tokyo, several years before his father, he had fallen in with a bad crowd and piled up gambling debts. Yoshihide began borrowing money from his father's disciples, which he did not pay back, and that naturally generated a great deal of resentment among the members of the Shotokan, causing his conscientious father no end of grief.

Despite this and other obstacles, after the war Funakoshi was able to pick up the shattered pieces and rebuild Shotokan karate. In 1949 the Japan Karate Association was formed (karate was the only martial art not banned by the Occupation Authorities, on the grounds that it was merely a kind of boxing and not a nationalistic budo), with Funakoshi as Chief Advisor. Funakoshi resumed his teaching activities, instructing again at his old university and at company dojo, while adding some new clubs.

Yet things were not the same. After the war Funakoshi admitted that he "became painfully aware of the almost unrecognizable spiritual state of present day karate." Then in his eighties, Funakoshi continued to emphasize *kata* training and karate ethics, but his classes were poorly attended, and would have been worse attended if white belts had not been required to participate. Young practitioners were interested in competition, in scoring points, in flashy movements. They did not take to being drilled in the fun-

温故古新自互規新之旧々
時推移人百芻争壹呉新
斯道改正誰伝宣
松濤

Calligraphy by Funakoshi: "Cherish the old while learning to understand the new; What is new, what is old, is simply a matter of time; Among myriad activities keep your mind clear; The way—who promises to attain it true and well." This piece is signed "Shoto," "Pine-Waves," Funakoshi's penname. The brushstrokes reveal Funakoshi's character: deeply refined and possessed of a quiet strength.

•

81

•

damentals and constantly admonished by an old man, even if that old man had an unsurpassed understanding of the real meaning of karate.

Funakoshi summed up his views on the art in his "Twenty Principles of Karate."

1. **Never forget that karate begins and ends with respect.** One must have respect for the teaching, respect for one's fellow trainees, and respect and reverence for life. "Respect" is one of the qualities that distinguishes a human being from a brute animal.

2. **There is no first attack in karate.** This is Funakoshi's best known maxim, and it is engraved on his tombstone. This principle is to be taken both literally ("If trouble comes, block your opponent's blows without striking in return; let him defeat himself") and figuratively ("Patience and fortitude are the marks of a true karate practitioner").

3. **Karate fosters righteousness.** When one is true to oneself, society as a whole benefits.

4. **First know yourself, and then know others.** Funakoshi learned this from his Master Azato: "If you know yourself and know your opponents well, you will never lose."

5. **Rather than physical technique, mental technique.** This is another version of "Technique does not make the person; the person make the technique."

6. **Let your mind roam freely.** This was the advice

Zen Master Takuan (1573–1645) gave to the swordsman Yagyu Munenori (1571–1646). If you allow your mind to settle anywhere, you lose your ability to respond. A free-ranging, nonstopping mind is the ideal.

7. **Inattention and neglect causes misfortune.** Most accidents in life are due to insufficient observation and pure laziness. Therefore a karate practitioner must always be alert. Funakoshi would always exercise caution when approaching corners, opening doors, and even when eating with chopsticks, taking care never to let his attention flag.

8. **Never think that karate is practiced only in the dojo.** The entire world is a dojo, and true karate training takes place twenty-four hours a day.

9. **Karate is a lifelong pursuit.** Near the end of his life, the eighty-year-old Funakoshi said of a certain karate movement he had been practicing for over sixty years, "I've finally got the hang of it!" It is said that on his deathbed, Funakoshi was still running *kata* through in his mind, trying to improve them.

10. **Everything you encounter is an aspect of karate; find the marvelous truth there.** The second half of this principle could also be translated, "karate is the spice of life."

11. **Karate is like boiling water; if you do not keep the flame high, it turns tepid.** Funakoshi told

his students, "For each day of practice you miss, the positive effects of three days previous training are lost."

12. **Do not think about winning; think about not losing.** There is a huge difference between wanting to win at all costs, and not allowing oneself to be defeated. The first approach leads to reckless destruction; the second fosters common sense and prudent action.

13. **Respond in accordance to your opponent.**

14. **Wage the battle with natural strategy.** That is, karate practitioners should act naturally when confronted with an attack, changing and adapting to their opponents, never forcing the issue.

15. **Regard your hands and feet as sharp swords.** This is not merely a matter of turning them into lethal weapons; it also makes the practitioner aware of their awesome potential.

16. **Step out the door and you face 10,000 foes.** This is another maxim that underlines the necessity of being vigilant at all times, taking nothing for granted.

17. **Learn various stances as a beginner, but then rely on a natural posture.** As a beginner, it is essential to learn various stances; such stances are the building blocks of karate. Eventually, however, a practitioner must transcend all conditioned stances

•

•

and assume the posture that is most natural and appropriate.

18. **The *kata* must always be practiced correctly; real combat is another matter.** The *kata* were devised to train different muscles, develop certain reflexes, and build stamina. Many—perhaps most—of the movements will never be utilized in real combat, but such *kata* provide the means to attain victory in real combat.

19. **Never forget your own strengths and weaknesses, the limitations of your body, and the relative quality of your techniques.** Again, if you know yourself well you are on the path to true victory.

20. **Continually polish your mind.** "Polish" here connotes constant research into the nature of things; such striving involves the whole person, and is a concentrated effort to remove all mental and physical obstacles that lie in one's path.

Funakoshi confessed that he himself once broke one of these rules. Not long after the end of the war, the old master was walking home at night along a deserted road. He was accosted by a robber, who demanded money and then cigarettes. When Funakoshi replied that he had neither, the robber grabbed Funakoshi's umbrella and tried to strike him with it. Funakoshi slipped pass the attack and seized the robber by the testicles, holding him firmly by the balls until the police showed up. The robber was obviously an amateur, most likely a desperate, unemployed veteran as Funakoshi surmised, and the karate master regretted not being able to defuse the situation before resorting to force.

After the war many foreigners began applying for permission to study karate. When a U.S. military officer asked Funakoshi to arrange a karate demonstration, the master replied (through a translator): "I will be happy to do so, but you must first make an application in writing and agree to wear your dress uniform when you attend the demonstration. I, too, will of course be in formal Japanese clothing." In other words, karate was not for show; it was a serious art.

Overseas interest in karate picked up considerably in the 1950s. The eighty-year-old Funakoshi, together with a

Eighty-year Funakoshi launching a lightening fast counterpunch in demonstration. The arm movement is a blur, but Funakoshi's stance is stable and settled. (Photo courtesy of Weatherhill.)

few of his top students, made a well-received instruction tour of American SAC bases in 1953. A film entitled *Karate-Do*, with English narration and briefly featuring Funakoshi, was issued in 1954 and distributed worldwide. Funakoshi's successors at the Shotokan, especially Masatoshi Nakayama (1913–1987), eventually spread the karate teachings of Funakoshi to all corners of the globe.

Funakoshi lived to be nearly ninety years of age. He attributed his longevity and good health to karate—"the best medicine there is"—and clean living. He never smoked, rarely drank, slept on a thin mat with a single blanket summer and winter, and bathed daily. In his autobiography, written a few years before his death, Funakoshi comes off as rather prissy and puritanical, but his young disciples relate in their memoirs that the old karate master was quite friendly and chatty outside of training, and he would often tease them about their love lives.

Funakoshi died on April 26, 1957. His long, fruitful life embodied the virtues of Shotokan karate: courage, courtesy, integrity, humility, and self-control.

Morihei Ueshiba

(1883–1969)

MORIHEI UESHIBA, ALTHOUGH BORN well into the modern era, more than twenty years later than Jigoro Kano, came to assume the proportions of a fantastic figure harking back to the Age of the Gods.

Ueshiba was born in Tanabe, Wakayama Prefecture. Several hundred miles south of Osaka, Tanabe is situated along the Pacific Ocean at the entrance to a pilgrim trail leading to the sacred mountains of Kumano. These holy mountains have been venerated since the dawn of Japanese history, and the landscape is dotted with ancient Shinto shrines, magnificent Buddhist temples, mysterious caves, and sacred falls. The area was originally called the "Province of Kii," and practitioners of Japanese-style *feng-sui* declare that the flow of cosmic energy there is likely the most powerful in the country. Throughout the centuries, wizards, wonder-workers, and warrior monks concealed themselves in the mountains of Kumano, abandoning themselves to ascetic training, seeking the secrets

•
91
•

of creation. Tales of their miracles abound, passed down from generation to generation among the local folk.

Here is a typical Kumano legend. A Buddhist priest, walking through a deep forest one morning, heard a heavenly chant drifting through the trees. After a long search, he discovered that the unearthly sound was emanating from deep inside a cave. Entering the cave, the priest found the skeletonized remains of a mountain ascetic fixed in the posture of meditation. The ascetic's tongue, however, was still vibrant, pouring forth the marvelous words of the sutras.

Yuki Ueshiba had already given birth to three girls, and she and her husband, Yoroku, desperately prayed for a son. The gods of Kumano answered their prayers on December 14, 1883. (They had one more child later, a daughter.) Although Morihei, as they called the boy, came from sturdy stock—both his grandfather and father were famed as strongmen—he was a small baby, perhaps a bit premature, and sickly as an infant. Even though he was to display superhuman strength later on, Ueshiba's constitution remained somewhat precarious throughout his life.

One of the oldest and most prominent families in Tanabe, the Ueshiba clan had substantial land holdings in the area as well as rights for shell-fishing along a portion of the bay. Yoroku served as a village council member for over twenty years. Ueshiba's mother, Yuki, enjoyed art and literature, and she was very pious. She arose at four o'clock every morning to worship at the main shrines in the village before beginning her day. From around the age of five Ueshiba accompanied her on this daily pilgrimage.

•

•

She also loved to tell her son the marvelous tales of the Kumano saints.

Ueshiba was an insatiably curious child with a photo-graphic memory. Like Kano and Funakoshi, his education began with the study of the Chinese classics. Since his teacher happened to be a Shingon priest, he received in-struction in the rites of esoteric Buddhism in addition to the Chinese texts. Ueshiba quickly became bored with dry Confucian doctrine, but he loved the rich texture of Shin-gon. The young Ueshiba was enthralled by the spectacular Shingon fire ceremony and the mystical chants, often reciting the words to various *mantra* in his sleep. He also gained experience in Shingon visualization techniques in which one mentally conjures up a deity and then attempts to merge with the image. From a young age, visions were a central part of his inner life.

Ueshiba was interested in books on mathematics and science, too, often becoming engrossed in experiments of his own design. Alarmed that his son was turning into a bookworm and inveterate dreamer, Yoroku had the boy take up sumo, hiking (to visit mountain shrines), and swimming. The ocean was only a two or three minute walk from the Ueshiba home, and during his years in Tana-be Ueshiba made it his practice to visit the ocean every day—as child to swim and spear fish, as a young man to perform religious ablutions. He spent most of his youth outdoors—by the ocean, in the fields, on the mountains. He thus came to understand and appreciate both the beneficence and the awesome power of nature. When his father was attacked one night by a group of thugs hired by

•

•

political opponents, Ueshiba discovered something about human nature—one must be strong enough to overcome brute force.

He loved books, enjoyed learning, but he hated class-rooms. Too impatient and high-strung to be cooped up in-doors all day, he persuaded his parents to let him drop out of middle school in his first year. He then studied at a *soro-ban* (abacus) academy where he could proceed at his own pace. Proving adept at calculation, he was acting as an as-sistant instructor at the academy within a year. Around 1900 he was hired as an accountant by the local Tax Bureau.

Not long after taking up his new position, however, he became involved in a protest movement against a newly enacted Fishery Regulation Law. Ueshiba believed that the law discriminated against local part-time fishermen who had to both farm and fish to make ends meet. He resigned his job in protest, joined the demonstrators, and became one of the leaders of the group opposing the new regula-tions. This proved embarrassing to Ueshiba's father, who, as a member of the village council, was bound to imple-ment the law.

Embittered when the protest movement fizzled out, Ueshiba was at a lost for what to do with his life. The fam-ily decided that a change of scene would do him good. With money provided by his father, the nineteen-year old Ueshiba left for Tokyo in the spring of 1902.

In Tokyo he apprenticed himself to a merchant for a few months and then, using a pushcart, peddled stationery and school supplies. He occupied his evenings by practic-ing Tenshin Shin'yo Ryu jujutsu and perhaps Shinkage

•
•

Ryu swordsmanship as well. This training did not last long, nor was it extensive, but it gave Ueshiba an inkling of his true calling—a warrior of the spirit.

Ueshiba's business went well, and he was able to hire several helpers. In the end, however, he developed a severe case of beriberi, no doubt brought on by the long hours of work and a poor diet, and turned the business over to his employees, asking nothing in return. Returning to Tanabe, he married Hatsu Itogawa, a distant relative on his mother's side, in October of 1902.

War between Russia and Japan was on the horizon, and Ueshiba knew that he would soon be drafted into the army. In order to recover his health and build up his body, he embarked on a rigorous training program. He spent long hours in the mountains swinging a heavy sword; he carried sick or injured pilgrims on his back over much of the twenty-mile path to Kumano Shrine, both as an act of charity and as a form of training; he worked on fishing boats to build up his arm strength; and similar to Funakoshi, he would go outside during typhoons to test himself against the surging waves and violent winds. Soon he was in tip-top physical condition and was thus appalled to be rejected by the army because of his height.

While not as short as Funakoshi, Ueshiba was only about 5'1½" tall. Since the minimum height for conscripts was 5'2", Ueshiba failed the initial examination. Many young men facing military service would have been relieved, but not Ueshiba. He wanted to join the army, he wanted to be a commander, he longed to be a hero. Intent on getting into the infantry, the determined young man took to hanging from trees with heavy weights on his legs in order to stretch his spine.

Persistence paid off, and he passed a supplementary examination and was assigned to the reserves stationed near Osaka. Ueshiba had resumed his practice of Shingon Buddhism after his return from Tokyo, and his teacher, the priest Mitsujo Fujimoto (d. 1947), conducted a special fire ceremony to mark his departure for military service. Following the ceremony, Mitsujo presented Ueshiba with a Shingon "Seal of Attainment" certificate. This triggered the first of a long series of mystical experiences for Ueshiba—"I felt as if a guardian deity had settled in the core of my being."

Although life in the Imperial Army was exceedingly harsh, Ueshiba relished the discipline. He was the first to volunteer for any task, however onerous (including latrine duty). During forced marches he would help stragglers by carrying their loads, but would still finish at he head of the pack. He also became extraordinarily skilled at bayonet fighting. During these army years Ueshiba made himself into a *tetsujin*, "a man of iron," weighing a massive 180 pounds.

Sometime during his time in the military, Ueshiba had enrolled in the dojo of Masakatsu Nakai (n.d.) in Sakai, a suburb of Osaka, where he trained on leave days. Nakai was an outstanding martial artist who taught Yagyu Ryu Jujutsu together with sword and spear arts. Nakai later became acquainted with Jigoro Kano, who held him in high regard and may have been his student. (Reportedly, a match was once held in Osaka between students of Nakai and members of the Kodokan, and Nakai's students won.) Ueshiba trained diligently under Nakai and another teacher named Tsuboi; he received a Goto-ha Yagyu Ryu Jujutsu teaching license from this school in 1908.

The Russo-Japanese War had commenced in earnest in 1904, but Ueshiba was kept back in the reserves. He insisted that he be sent to the front, and in 1905 he was assigned to a regiment departing for Manchuria. It is not clear how much action Ueshiba saw. His father had secretly written several letters to the military authorities, requesting that his only son be kept away from the front, and Ueshiba is unlikely to have engaged in any hand-to-hand fighting.

Thus Ueshiba returned from the war unscathed. Not surprisingly, considering his gung-ho attitude, several of his superiors recommended that he enroll in the Military Officers Training School. Having attained the rank of staff sergeant, Ueshiba considered the possibility, but his father was steadfastly against it. He was therefore discharged from the army and went home to Tanabe.

The next few years were very trying. He had yet to find his niche in life, and the stress of not knowing where to turn next began to tell. He would shut himself up in his room to pray for hours or would disappear into the woods for days at a time. Prone to anguished outbursts, Ueshiba's family worried about his sanity. His father built a dojo on family property and encouraged his son to train his cares away. This helped a bit, and in 1909 Ueshiba came under the beneficial influence of Kumakusu Minakata (1867–1941).

•

•

Ueshiba was attracted to unusual characters, and Minakata was a world-class eccentric. Among the first group of Japanese to travel overseas, Minakata had lived in the United States, the West Indies, and then settled in England, where he acted as a lecturer of Japanese Studies at Cambridge. After eighteen years abroad, Minakata returned to his hometown of Tanabe in 1904 and immediately got embroiled in the "Shrine Consolation Act" controversy. The Meiji government planned to consolidate as many shrines as possible and then appropriate the land of smaller shrines for "development." Minakata, who was also well known as a naturalist, vehemently opposed the Act since he knew it would result in the destruction of much of the natural beauty of the area and irrevocably alter the folk culture of Wakayama. Minakata and Ueshiba teamed up to lead the protest movement, which proved effective—only one-fifth of the shrines in Wakayama were confiscated in the end, and Tanabe itself only lost six out of nearly a hundred shrines.

Working for a righteous cause raised Ueshiba's spirits, and Minakata encouraged him to set his sights higher still. Ueshiba realized that his future was not in Tanabe. The area was too mountainous to support any more rice paddies, and the harbor was full of all the fishing boats it could hold and that the law allowed; many jobless young people had already left for greener pastures, some immigrating as far afield as Hawaii or the West Coast of the United States. When a call was issued for volunteer settlers to the northernmost island of Hokkaido, Ueshiba decided to become a pioneer.

•

•

Following a preliminary inspection tour to Hokkaido in 1910, Ueshiba came back convinced that it was a virgin land full of promise. Over the next two years, he was able to recruit eighty-four people who were willing to gamble on a move to Shirataki, a well-watered, fertile area Ueshiba had scouted during his initial trip. While enthusiastic, the group lacked sufficient resources, and Ueshiba's ever generous father put up the money for the entire party. They set off for Hokkaido on March 29, 1912. (Ueshiba's wife, who had given birth in 1911 to their first child, a daughter, would join her husband in Hokkaido somewhat later.)

The Shirataki site lay deep in the center of vast Hokkaido, and it was not an easy journey there from mild Wakayama. Slowed down by blizzards, the group did not reach its destination until the twentieth of May. Being a pioneer was a hard business, and the settlers found the first three years in Shirataki to be brutal. The harvests were poor, the climate frigid, and outside help nonexistent. The group subsisted on wild mountain vegetables, nuts, and river fish. After this initial period of unremitting hardship, income from lumbering operations began to increase, farming skills improved, and a genuine village started to form. Inspired by these challenges, Ueshiba's spirits never sank; he was ever the driving force behind the settlement. He was a tireless entrepreneur, instrumental in introducing lumbering, mint farming, and hog raising, and a dedicated citizen who organized health and sanitation brigades and served as a village council member. A great fire in 1916, which destroyed eighty percent of the buildings, proved a temporary setback, but thanks to Ueshiba's ceaseless efforts, the Hokkaido settlement project was, all in all, a great success.

Ueshiba kept up his religious practices, primarily *misogi*, ritual ablutions with cold water, which was no mean feat in the deathly cold of Hokkaido. At first, his martial art training consisted mostly of wrestling the huge logs he had cut down with a specially weighted heavy ax—in one season Ueshiba is supposed to have single-handedly felled and chopped up 500 trees. He also engaged in impromptu sumo contests and other matches fought with wooden bayonets. He had to deal with highwaymen on occasion, but those confrontations were easily dealt with by someone with Ueshiba's martial art experience. He had a few run-ins with big Hokkaido bears, but he somehow managed to placate the beasts. Ueshiba was supremely confident of his strength and skill—that is, until he faced Sokaku Takeda, Grandmaster of the Daito Ryu.

Sokaku Takeda (1860–1943) may well have been the premier martial artist of his day. Probably neither Kano nor Funakoshi would have been much of a match for Takeda, who had acquired his fearsome skill by fighting one battle after another in dojo and streets all over Japan. Takeda had been born in Aizu, home of perhaps the fiercest samurai in the country. His father, Sokichi (1819–1906), was a sumo champion as well as master of sword and spear arts, and from a very early age Sokaku had learned how to fight in the family dirt-floored dojo. Even after the feudal order collapsed following the Meiji Restoration in 1868, Takeda acted like an old-time warrior. He set off on a long journey, which eventually covered the length and breath of Japan, to train under, and challenge, the best budo masters still living, and to test himself against all comers.

For some years following the Meiji Restoration, law and order had largely broken down, and Takeda had plenty of opportunities to prove his mettle against bandits and gangsters. He liked nothing better than giving brigands a thrashing, not a few of whom died of their injuries. In 1877 Takeda attempted to join the rebellious forces of Saigo Takamori in Kyushu. That plan was thwarted when the rebellion was crushed before Takeda could enlist, but he spent two years in Kyushu and Okinawa honing his skills in challenges against local karate men. (Since karate was still practiced in secret during this time, most of these encounters must have been street fights.) Some sources claim that Takeda even paid a visit to the rowdy ports of Hawaii.

Periodically Takeda would return to Fukushima to study the secret *oshiki-uchi* techniques of the Aizu clan under the direction of Tanomo Saigo (1872–1923). Tanomo had also taught these techniques to his adopted (some say illegitimate) son Shiro Saigo, who played such an important role in the early days of the Kodokan. It is not clear exactly what *oshiki-uchi* encompassed (after all, it was secret), but the *oshiki-uchi* teachings likely emphasized samurai etiquette as much as martial art techniques. Eventually Takeda combined the core elements of *oshiki-uchi* with techniques derived from his unparalleled practical experience of classical budo and actual combat to form what he called Daito Ryu Aikijutsu.

Takeda led a peripatetic life, often on the fringes of society, wandering to and fro in remote areas of Northern
Japan. If he had based himself in a big urban area such as
Tokyo or Osaka, an organization might have developed
around him to rival the Kodokan in size and influence.
Considering that he spent most of his life teaching in the
district known as the "Tibet of Japan," the number of
prominent military officers and government officials who
were registered as Takeda's students is most impressive.
U.S. President Teddy Roosevelt, whose enthusiasm for
Japanese jujutsu was noted previously, got wind of Takeda's remarkable prowess from an American who had
the misfortune of challenging Takeda to a fight. Conse-
quently, a student of Takeda's named Hara was dispatched
to teach in the United States. (Further details, unfortunately, are lacking.)

Takeda himself shunned the limelight, preferring to se-
clude himself from the world, and frequently his where-
abouts were unknown. Without formal education, he often
uttered the blasphemy, "The notion that budo and deep
learning are of equal value to a samurai is nonsense. Book
learning is useless!" He was obsessively suspicious and
had his disciples sample his food and drink to ensure that
it was not poisoned. Takeda was a difficult, demanding
man.

Nevertheless, given his success in battling outlaws, he
was in great demand as a special instructor to outlying police departments that had to deal with aggressive criminal
gangs. Takeda's talents were particularly valuable in Hok-

kaido, which was then much like the American "Wild West," a vast, untamed frontier teaming with fugitives from justice. Although Takeda had been living in Hokkaido since around 1910, Ueshiba did not meet him until 1915. (Hokkaido remained Takeda's base until 1930. He married a spunky young girl thirty years his junior, who bore him seven children in addition to acting as an assistant Daito Ryu instructor. She died in a tragic fire in 1930.)

Ueshiba was introduced to Takeda by Kentaro Yoshida (1886–1964), another peculiar fellow. Yoshida was a well-known supporter of various right-wing causes, and he had lived in the United States for some time, perhaps operating as a spy. The Daito Ryu training was being conducted at an inn in Engaru, the largest village in the area. As soon as Ueshiba saw Takeda in action, he was hooked and enrolled at once in the ten-day course.

Takeda had not inherited the physique of his sumo champion father. He was tiny, less than five feet tall, and he was thin. His extraordinary ability was due to technical perfection, immaculate timing, mind control, and mastery of *ki* power. *Ki* was the key to budo; it was an inexhaustible fount of energy and power—Takeda could throw any number of attackers through *aiki*, the subtle blending of positive and negative energy. Ueshiba was entranced by Takeda's performance, and he signed up for another ten-day course immediately after completing the first. Thereafter Ueshiba trained with Takeda as much as possible, accompanying the master on teaching tours and inviting him to stay at the Ueshiba home.

•

•

When Takeda stayed with the Ueshibas, Morihei would rise at 2:30 A.M. to prepare a morning bath for his teacher. He would kindle a fire to warm Takeda's room and then make breakfast. Ueshiba washed Takeda's back in the bath, served him breakfast afterward, and then massaged him for an hour. In return, Ueshiba got private lessons, lessons which were both unrelentingly severe and of inestimable value.

Ueshiba had benefited much from the move to Hokkaido. He had been invigorated by the challenge of creating something out of nothing as a pioneer. He had been a success as a farmer and as an entrepreneur, and he proved himself to be a responsible citizen. He had flourished in the vast wilderness and built up tremendous strength and stamina. He had learned budo from the best martial artist in the land. Despite all this, however, Ueshiba was restless: he had always been searching for something more than material success or mere prowess as a martial artist. He longed for something deeper, some purpose more enduring. In December of 1919 a telegram arrived, informing him that his father was gravely ill. Ueshiba gave his house to Takeda, divided up his property and possessions, and left Hokkaido for good.

He did not return directly to Tanabe. Something drew him instead to Ayabe, headquarters of Omoto-kyo. Omoto-kyo was one of the "new religions" founded during the upheavals that sweep over Japan during the last half of the nineteenth and the beginning of the twentieth centuries. These new religions were mostly messianic in nature, and Omoto-kyo was championing the "Buddha

Who Is to Come," Onisaburo Deguchi (1871–1947).

Of all the colorful characters that Ueshiba encountered during his eventful life, Deguchi was undoubtedly the most charismatic and controversial. The Omoto-kyo religion had actually been founded by Nao Deguchi (1836–1918), a miserably poor peasant woman turned shaman. Onisaburo married Nao's daughter Sumi and eventually took control of the organization, molding it to his own image. For Deguchi—who claimed to have spent seven days roaming the vast reaches of the universe, calling on every deity known to humankind—that image was aggressively prophetic, elegantly esthetic, and wildly flamboyant.

Perhaps hoping for a miracle that would save his dying father, Ueshiba participated in a prayer service at the main hall of the Omoto-kyo compound. A vision of his father appeared to him during the service, a figure thin and diaphanous. Suddenly Deguchi himself came up to Ueshiba and asked, "What have you seen?" "My father," Ueshiba replied. "He was so …" "He will be fine," Deguchi reassured him. "Let him go."

Ueshiba stayed several more days in Ayabe learning about Omoto-kyo, and the more he learned the more he was fascinated by the religion. By the time he arrived in Tanabe his father was already dead. His relatives were understandably upset with him for not arriving sooner. Nonetheless his father had passed away peacefully, leaving his son these final words: "Do not be constrained; live the way you really want." When he heard these words, Ueshiba grabbed his sword and headed for the mountains.

In the early part of his life, Ueshiba would go up into the mountains whenever troubled and spend hours wildly swinging his sword. Following his father's death, he did so with such intensity that the police were asked to arrest the "wild man with the sword." Fortunately, the police chief, who had served under Ueshiba in the army, recognized the distraught mourner and Ueshiba escaped arrest. He eventually regained his senses, but when he announced his intention to move to Ayabe and join Omoto-kyo, his family thought he must be genuinely crazy. The Ueshibas had two children (a son had been born to them in Hokkaido), and they were expecting another. Ueshiba was also now responsible for the care of his mother. "What do you mean the gods are calling you?" Ueshiba's wife demanded, "Are those gods going to pay you a salary?" Ueshiba's mind was made up, however, and early in 1920 the entire family made the move to Ayabe.

It is easy to understand the reasons for Ueshiba's infatuation with Deguchi. His quest had always been primarily spiritual rather than martial, and Omoto-kyo afforded him a sound framework within which to work toward the goal of "total awakening." Deguchi had formulated a number of effective meditation techniques and powerful chants based on *kototama* ("sound-spirit") theory. He also taught his followers that "Art is the essence of religion"; the goal of Omoto-kyo was to turn all daily actions into works of art. Everyone was encouraged to be a poet, a singer, a calligrapher, a potter, a weaver, a chef. Food was homegrown, fresh and organic. The theology was cosmic; all religions emanated from the same source, and the nations of the world would gradually draw closer together. Most important of all, Ueshiba and Deguchi were on the same spiritual wavelength: Ueshiba was spared all cumbersome organizational duties and given the freedom to bring his own special art to full fruition.

Deguchi believed Ueshiba's destiny to be the revelation of the true meaning of budo to the world. A dojo was constructed in the compound, and the thirty-six-year-old Ueshiba began teaching budo to members of Omoto-kyo. The first year the Ueshiba family spent in Ayabe, however, was not at all auspicious. Both of Ueshiba's sons died of illness in 1920, and then in February of 1921 Ayabe was raided by government agents.

The Japanese authorities had been keeping a close watch on Deguchi's activities for some time. Although Japan at that time was full of would-be messiahs, the government dismissed most of them as harmless crackpots. Deguchi, however, was different: he had gathered around him a large group of influential supporters, he had a nationwide network of dedicated Omoto-kyo members, and he had started up a newspaper to disseminate his radical ideas to the general public. He was a spell-binding speaker and a master showman, and while the threat of Deguchi actually overthrowing the government and proclaiming himself emperor was slight, the nervous authorities were taking no chances. Deguchi was charged with *lese majesty*, arrested, and convicted. He was released on bond four months later, but while he was in prison the Omoto-kyo compound was ransacked and burned to the ground by government order. Never one to be deterred, Deguchi

Morihei Ueshiba, around the age of thirty-eight, when he was teaching budo at the Omoto-kyo compound in Ayabe. Ueshiba had moved there in 1920 to study under the Shinto shaman Onisaburo Deguchi. (All photos of Morihei courtesy of Kisshomaru Ueshiba.)

began rebuilding immediately after his release from jail.

Ueshiba was not seriously affected by this "First Omoto-kyo Incident." He was a new member and not under government surveillance, and he had wisely purchased a three-year supply of rice before coming to Ayabe, thus allowing his family to survive during the crackdown. In June of 1921, Ueshiba's third and sole surviving son, Kisshomaru, was born.

Around the end of April in 1922, Takeda, accompanied by his wife and family, arrived in Ayabe. Whether Takeda was invited by Ueshiba or simply showed up on his own accord is a matter of contention; at any rate, he stayed about four months, giving instruction in Daito Ryu Aiki Jujutsu. Deguchi took an immediate dislike to him— "The man reeks of blood and violence"—and Takeda made no secret of his contempt for Omoto-kyo beliefs. Takeda departed Ayabe in September after certifying Ueshiba as a full-fledged Daito Ryu instructor.

Ueshiba continued to teach and train at Ayabe, and he spent many nights practicing outdoors with a sword and a spear: he hung sponge balls in the branches of the trees near the dojo and practiced spearing them in rapid succession. In addition to his duties as a budo instructor, Ueshiba was put in charge of the extensive Omoto-kyo organic gardens. His days began at 3:00 A.M., when he rose to gather fertilizer and work the fields.

In February of 1924, Deguchi, his bodyguard Ueshiba, and several others left Japan secretly and embarked on the "great Mongolian Adventure." Deguchi, always reaching for the stars, dreamed of establishing a "Heaven on Earth" in Mongolia. Various Japanese schemers operating in China supported Deguchi's plans, believing that it would be easier to take control of the area if some charismatic religious figure first won the people's hearts. Although Deguchi was aware that right-wing conspirators were trying to use him for their own purposes, he was confident he could turn the tables and establish a real "Peaceable Kingdom of the New Jerusalem," not a puppet colonial government.

In China Deguchi and his party linked up with a man called Yano, an espionage agent and gun runner, and a Chinese bandit leader named Lu. Deguchi declared himself the "Rising Sun Dalai Lama," and the group made their way to Inner Mongolia. The notion of a Heaven on Earth was familiar to the Mongolians—they called it "Shambhala"—and since they also believed in the coming of Miroku Buddha to save the world, Deguchi, playing his part to the hilt, created a sensation among pious Buddhist believers. The reception the Deguchi group received from local war lords, bandits, and the Chinese army was considerably less warm, with the group frequently coming under fire. Fortunately for Ueshiba, he was blessed with a miraculous sixth sense that enabled him to divine the direction of the bullets. When he wasn't keeping clear of gunfire, Ueshiba was obliged to fight off attackers in deadly hand-to-hand combat. Near the end of the journey, the lives of the men in the Deguchi group were constantly in danger, and Ueshiba sat up all night next to Deguchi to protect his master.

Alas, the time was not ripe for heaven to appear on

earth. Lu and all 130 of his men were captured and executed by the Chinese army. The Japanese "agitators" were bound and led to the same blood-soaked execution ground. Deguchi and his group sang their farewell verses and calmly awaited their fate. The Chinese riflemen dithered for some reason, and then there was a reprieve— the Deguchi group was to be released into the custody of the Japanese consul. In July 1924 Deguchi and Ueshiba returned safely to Japan.

There Deguchi was rearrested for violating the conditions of bail, whereas Ueshiba was free to return to Ayabe. While wandering the vast, mysterious plains of Mongolia, Ueshiba had been continually face-to-face with death, and cutthroat foes had perished at his hands. Such wrenching experiences made Ueshiba a changed man. Training with an intensity greater than ever, Ueshiba armed his students with live blades and commanded them to try to cut him down. People near Ueshiba could sense an awesome power swirling about him, and objects in a room would rattle when he entered. During this period, Ueshiba wandered about a great deal, as far south as Kumamoto, and apparently underwent *yamabushi* austerities in and around Nachi Falls in Kumano.

In the spring of 1925, a navy officer renowned for his skill in kendo visited Ueshiba at the Ayabe dojo. A disagreement arose about the finer points of budo, and Ueshiba invited the officer to try to strike him with a wooden sword. Enraged by what he took as impudence, the officer lashed out without the slightest reserve. The unarmed Ueshiba avoided even the quickest strikes, perceiving each attack as a beam of light. After the officer collapsed, exhausted in defeat, Morihei went out into the garden to dowse his face with cold water from the well and to collect his thoughts.

As he was walking among the trees, Ueshiba felt the ground tremble beneath his feet, and he was enveloped in golden rays. Suffused with light, he lost all sense of time and place, and then, suddenly, everything appeared clear and bright. "I saw the divine," he later said, describing the experience, "and attained an enlightenment that was true, self-conquering, swift and sure. All at once I understood the nature of creation: the way of a warrior is to manifest divine love, a spirit that embraces and nutures all things. Tears of gratitude and joy streamed down my cheeks. I saw the entire universe as my home, and the sun, moon, and stars as my intimate friends. All attachment to things material vanished."

Following this earth-shattering transformation, Ueshiba began to manifest incredible powers: he could displace enormous boulders, leap unbelievable distances, and dispose of any kind of attack—anywhere, anytime. Naturally, such amazing feats attracted the attention of people outside Omoto-kyo circles.

A young judo man named Nishimura, interested in Omoto-kyo teachings, stopped by the Ayabe compound and met Deguchi. Learning that Nishimura was captain of the Waseda University Judo Club, the mischievous Omoto-kyo leader said, "We have a fellow here who brags of being the top martial artist in Japan. Why don't you show him some judo and teach him a thing or two?"

Nishimura, a large and powerful man in his early twenties, nearly sneered in derision when introduced to Ueshiba. He thought to himself, "What? This little country bumpkin claims to be the best in Japan? I'll crush him!" Moving in on Ueshiba, Nishimura suddenly and inexplicably found himself sitting on his rear end. Getting to his feet, he went after Ueshiba several more times, only to meet with similar results. As he looked up at Ueshiba's beaming face, Nishimura marveled, "What a great thing—a martial art in which one is thrown with a smile."

Nishimura told his friends about Ueshiba, and rumors of the "wizard of Ayabe" spread. In the autumn of 1925 Admiral Isamu Takeshita—who acted as a patron to Kano, Funakoshi, and now Ueshiba—organized a demonstration in Tokyo for a select group of dignitaries. The demonstration was a big hit. Ueshiba awed the crowd by, among other things, spearing 125-pound sacks of rice and flipping them about without spilling a single grain. As a result, he was invited to teach a twenty-one day course at Aoyama Palace for high-ranking judo and kendo instructors.

Although the seminar was successfully concluded, certain officials objected to Ueshiba's presence at any kind of government-sponsored event because of his close ties to the controversial Deguchi. Offended by the insinuations, Ueshiba returned to Ayabe. Deguchi, however, encouraged him to disassociate himself from Omoto-kyo and set out on his own unique path. He reminded Ueshiba, "Your purpose in life is to reveal the true meaning of budo to the world."

•

•

In 1926 Ueshiba was persuaded by Admiral Takeshita to return to Tokyo. He quickly developed a following among military men and was supported by several wealthy patrons. It was then, however, that Ueshiba's health failed, as he succumb to stomach and liver disorders. He returned to Ayabe to recuperate, but six months later he was back in Tokyo, this time for good. His family joined him in September of 1927.

Between 1927 and 1931, Ueshiba taught at several makeshift dojo—one was the remodeled billiard room of a villa owned by Duke Shimazu. His students were high-ranking army and navy officers, aristocrats, and wealthy businessmen. Many of these men had their daughters train as well, and thus a number of women were always present in the dojo. Ueshiba continued to dazzle the sophisticated Tokyoites. Once at a military base, he took on an entire platoon, some forty men in total, and threw them all in rapid succession. More and more people clamored for instruction.

Still, it was difficult for many to believe that Ueshiba was the real thing. Once a newspaperman named Ishii visited the dojo in Mita for training. No one else was there, and during the lesson Ueshiba brought out a spear. He told Ishii to thrust at him with full force, "So I can show you how to handle such attacks." Ishii, however, was reluctant, "What if I hit you, and you die? There are no eyewitnesses and I could be charged with murder." "No, it's all right," Morihei reassured him; "nothing will happen." Ishii couldn't bring himself to truly attack, though, and nothing came of the incident.

•

•

Others, however, were not hesitant to have a try at Ueshiba. General Miura, a student of Sokaku Takeda and a hero of the Russo-Japanese War (despite having been run through the chest with a bayonet, he managed to fight off a charge of enemy soldiers), launched a murderous attack, but ended up on the ground, completely immobilized. After making a sincere apology for his presumptuousness, Miura requested to be accepted as a disciple.

Ueshiba's students helped to spread the reputation of their remarkable teacher. Women were filled with admiration when they heard tales of tiny girls routing ugly mashers. After they were defeated by Ueshiba's smaller and lighter students, sumo wrestlers and judo men clamored to learn more about this new style of budo.

After hearing so much about Ueshiba from his Kodokan students, the ever eager researcher Jigoro Kano requested a demonstration. In October of 1930 Kano visited the temporary dojo in Mejiro and was dazzled by Ueshiba's performance: "This is my ideal budo; it is true and genuine judo." Kano had repeatedly explained to his Kodokan students that the key theory of judo was, "When your partner comes, greet him; when he departs, send him on his way." Ueshiba said the same thing to his trainees, but he could actually demonstrate such a feat regardless of the attack employed. After the demonstration, Kano sent Ueshiba a letter of appreciation and asked him to teach several advanced students from the Kodokan.

A number of Kodokan Judo men trained under Ueshiba, and several of them even switched entirely to

•

•

Ueshiba Ryu Jujutsu, as the art was then sometimes called (it was also called Aiki-Budo). One fellow, a judo sixth *dan* named Tetsuo Hoshi (d. 1947) actually returned his rank to the Kodokan after being tossed about by Ueshiba. "I didn't feel any physical power present," Hoshi told friends, "but I still kept on landing stretched out on the mat." Deadly earnest about training, Hoshi once nearly caught Ueshiba off guard. Ueshiba was teaching him some basic *aiki* moves when Hoshi suddenly grabbed his teacher and attempted to throw him. Ueshiba managed to recover in the nick of time and neutralize the throw. He was not angry with Hoshi, who was just being a martial artist ready to seize any opening; rather he was upset with himself for being slack. Ueshiba learned a valuable lesson from the incident. "Even with one's disciples, you should never take anything for granted and let your guard down." (During World War II the undisciplined and unprincipled Hoshi practiced his techniques on foreign captives, and he was eventually executed as a war criminal.)

In 1931 a permanent *dojo* and living quarters for Ueshiba was built in the Wakamatsu-cho section of Tokyo. For the next ten years the Kobukan ("Hall of Majestic Martial Arts") was to be the center of a whirlwind of activities. Sokaku Takeda visited the Kobukan for a few weeks in early spring, but after this Ueshiba and Takeda parted ways. Ueshiba began accepting full-time live-in trainees (*uchi-deshi*) at the Kobukan, although he was quite selective about whom he admitted. Prospective disciples needed two sponsors well-known to Ueshiba, and the candidate had to pass an unsettling interview with the master. In such interviews the candidate would be invited to attack Ueshiba, "any way you like," which inevitably resulted in the candidate flying ten or so feet through the air and crashing to the mat.

Since Ueshiba was so choosy, the number of live-in disciples during this period was never large—usually averaging around ten trainees camping out in the dojo with perhaps a similar number of students who lived in the immediate neighborhood. Reportedly, Kano told Ueshiba, "You are doing the right thing. The Kodokan has grown too big, and it is out of my control." There were also several noteworthy full-time women trainees at Kobukan.

Particularly outstanding was Takako Kunigoshi (b. 1909). She was famed for her ability to hold her own even against the biggest and strongest men trainees, such as Rinjiro Shirata (1912–93). Shirata, the Kobukan *uchi-deshi* usually assigned to deal with any challengers who turned up when Ueshiba was absent, said of the charming Miss Kunigoshi: "I never faced a tougher opponent." She did the drawings for Ueshiba's first manual, *Budo Renshu*, privately circulated in 1933. (Another book by Ueshiba, entitled *Budo* and illustrated with photographs, was published in 1938.)

Ueshiba became the budo teacher of the nation's elite. He taught at all the principal military academies in Tokyo, he gave lessons to members of the Imperial household (the Emperor himself did not practice, but one of his brothers took lessons from Ueshiba), and he visited Osaka frequently to train police officers and military men there. A number of wealthy men trained at the Kobukan, and in

Ueshiba (left) demonstrating an *aiki* technique with Yoshimi Yonekawa (b. 1910). Ueshiba favored seated techniques, believing that they built up leg and hip power better than any other exercise. This is one in a series of photographs shot in the Noma Dojo in 1936, when Ueshiba was fifty-three years old.

addition to obtaining substantial donations from those supporters, Ueshiba eventually received a salary from the government that was nearly equal to that of a cabinet minister.

Near the end of 1935 the government again cracked down on Omoto-kyo, this time determined to silence the troublesome Deguchi once and for all and suppress the activities of his subversive followers. More than 500 Omoto-kyo members were arrested in the initial raid, and a warrant was issued for Ueshiba as well. Even though Ueshiba had loosened his ties to Omoto-kyo since his move to Tokyo, he headed the Dai-Nihon Budo Sen'yo Kai, an association established in 1932 to promote the practice of martial arts among Omoto-kyo followers; further, several key members of the Sakura Kai, an ultra-nationalist group of young military officers who had conspired to overthrow the government in 1931, had once used the Kobukan as a meeting ground. As a result of these compromising relationships, Ueshiba had been under government surveillance since he first began teaching in Tokyo in 1925. Ueshiba was not involved in any of the various plots being hatched by people around him but officers at the Kyoto Police Headquarters were nonetheless insistent on Ueshiba's detainment. He was in Osaka when the raid took place, and fortunately for him the police chief of Osaka, Kenji Tomita (d. 1977), was one of his disciples. Tomita managed to convince the Kyoto police not to arrest Ueshiba without further investigation, and another disciple, who was the police chief of Sonezaki, concealed Ueshiba in his home. In Tokyo, Kiyoshi Nakakura

(b. 1910), then Ueshiba's son-in-law, burned all Omoto-kyo related material and objects in the dojo and at the Ueshiba residence, in case there should be a police search. Nakakura thought that his father-in-law would be furious at the destruction of scrolls and other things written by Deguchi, but Ueshiba said nothing when he returned safely to Tokyo.

It also seems that Deguchi himself declared to the authorities that Ueshiba was not a member of the inner circle of the Omoto-kyo organization, and following a tense period of uncertainty, Ueshiba was free to begin instructing again in public. There are many fantastic tales told about Ueshiba during this period, perhaps the most incredible being the "Firing Range Showdown."

There was an impeccable eyewitness to this amazing feat, a certain Gozo Shioda (1915–94). The skeptical Shioda was not an Omoto-kyo believer and never uncritically accepted anything about Ueshiba. With Ueshiba's encouragement, for instance, Shioda was constantly trying to catch his teacher off guard. During long train rides Ueshiba would hand Shioda his iron fan and tell him, "If you can hit me with this while I'm napping, I'll give you a full teaching license." Whenever Ueshiba appeared to have dozed off, Shioda would prepare to strike. Exactly at that moment Ueshiba's eyes would pop open. "Shioda! The gods told me that you are planning to whack me over the head. You wouldn't be thinking something like that, would you?"

One day a group of military marksmen visited the Kobukan to watch a demonstration. When Ueshiba found out who they were, he provokingly said, "Bullets cannot touch me." The marksmen were understandably offended and challenged him to prove himself. Ueshiba agreed to sign a release form, absolving the marksmen of all liability in case he was shot and killed, and a date was set for Ueshiba to come to their firing range. Shioda had first-hand experience of his teacher's amazing powers, but he later confessed that he privately thought, "This time he has gone too far. We'd better start preparing for Master Ueshiba's funeral."

On the day of the showdown Ueshiba's wife pleaded with him not to go through with it. Ueshiba told her not to worry, and off he went to the firing range, seemingly without a care in the world. At the range he calmly placed himself as the target some seventy-five feet from six marksmen. As they aimed and fired, several of them were immediately knocked off their feet, and Ueshiba inexplicably stood unharmed *behind* them. Everyone was dumbstruck and asked Ueshiba to repeat the miracle. "Of course," he replied and once more set himself up as the target, again seventy-five feet away. Aware that something supernatural was about to occur, Shioda glued his eyes to Ueshiba's figure. The guns went off, the marksmen went flying, and again Ueshiba ended up behind everybody, laughing. Shioda had not been able to discern a single thing.

On the way back, Shioda asked his teacher, "How on earth did you do that?" Ueshiba replied cryptically, "My purpose on earth is not finished yet, so nothing can kill me. Once my task is completed, then it will be time to go.

•

•

Until then, I'm perfectly safe from all harm." (The above miracle somewhat resembles that told of Jesus, "slipping through the lynch mob and walking away unhurt," in Luke 4:30.)

Perhaps because the time itself was so turbulent, Ueshiba was not infrequently possessed by the gods of wrath. His temper was explosive, and his anger cowed even the most powerful men—after committing some transgression a live-in disciple spent an entire day with his head bowed to the floor in abject apology. Late one night, on another occasion, Ueshiba burst into the dojo in a fury, brandishing a wooden sword; the live-in disciples leaped up in confusion as Ueshiba decapitated a large rat who was nibbling the food offerings placed on the dojo shrine. Then Ueshiba berated the disciples for their inexcusable inattention and sloth. Luckily, Ueshiba's wrath would dissipate as quickly as it arose, and he would reassure his disciples, "Don't take it personally. It was just the gods expressing their brief displeasure."

After escaping from the police dragnet cast over the Omoto-kyo organization, and following the death of Kano in 1938, Ueshiba emerged as the senior budo instructor in Japan. His students occupied many of the top posts in the government and the military. He also became heavily involved in the Japanese administration of Manchukuo, the puppet government set up in Manchuria in 1932, frequently teaching there and becoming, in effect, the Chief Martial Arts Advisor of the Manchukuo government.

Full-scale war had broken out in China in 1937, and Pearl Harbor was attacked in 1941. (It is rumored that this

Ueshiba demonstrating his incredible *aiki* power as an old man of eighty-three. Once a Japanese professional baseball player swung a bat full force against Ueshiba's outstretched wooden sword. Upon impact, his bat flew back in the opposite direction, while Ueshiba's sword remained perfectly still.

bombing raid, primarily planned by the Imperial Navy, was based on the Aiki-Budo principle of *irimi-tenkan*—seize the initiative and then circle behind the enemy.) Ueshiba was reportedly sent on a secret peace mission to China in 1942. Due to his extensive contacts and his high repute among military and civil leaders, it was hoped that Ueshiba would be able to conclude a peace treaty between China and Japan. Nothing came of his efforts, alas, and the war continued unabated to its terrible conclusion.

The war placed a tremendous strain on Ueshiba. He complained of the brutality and ignorance of many in the armed forces, and later confided to his disciples that he detested teaching at the Espionage and Military Police Academies. The violence and destruction of war was contrary to the express purpose of true budo: to foster and promote life. In 1942 Ueshiba resigned all his official positions, pleading illness, and withdrew to his farm in Iwama.

From around 1938 Ueshiba had been acquiring land in Iwama, a village about two hours by train from Tokyo. Throughout his life, Ueshiba had been nurtured most by being out under the vast sky, walking along the deep ocean, or training among the high peaks. He was not city-bred, and he longed for the country, the fresh air and clean living, throughout the period he was stuck in crowded, concrete Tokyo. Ueshiba moved into a little shack on the property with his wife, far away from the fighting. He was not insensitive to the dreadful suffering that was taking place all over Asia, however. He was deathly ill several times during this time, a sickness that was both real and

•

•

symbolic. In order to recuperate, and to prepare for the renewal of Japan, Ueshiba starting practicing what he now called aikido—"the Art of Peace."

Japan surrendered in August of 1945. Although Tokyo was in ruins, the Kobukan Dojo remained intact owing to the heroic efforts of Ueshiba's son Kisshomaru. All martial arts (with the exception of karate, as mentioned previously) were banned by the Occupation, however, and the Kobukan Foundation was dissolved. Ueshiba remained in seclusion at his Aiki Garden in Iwama, farming, praying, and preparing himself to introduce aikido to the world.

Conditions were grim after Japan's defeat. Many of Ueshiba's former students had perished in the fighting, and the survivors were too busy eking out a living to take up training. The Tokyo dojo was occupied by squatters (the building was also said to have served briefly as a dance hall for Occupation troops). However, as Japan slowly began to rebuild, Ueshiba's students and supporters regrouped to form the Aikikai Foundation in 1948. The ban on the practice of budo was lifted, and around 1950 regular practice of aikido resumed.

A new order was needed, and Ueshiba's grand vision of aikido as a non-competitive art that fostered spiritual and physical well-being seemed to be ideal. A fresh generation of eager students began training within a few years after the end of the war, and during the 1950s the art of aikido was introduced to the world at large, with Ueshiba's son Kisshomaru handling the organizational details. In the early part of this decade, aikido was introduced to France and Hawaii by Japanese instructors, and by the mid-fifties foreign trainees from various countries around the globe were regular participants in Tokyo dojo training.

The first public demonstration of aikido was held on the roof of a Tokyo department store in September of 1955. This was a highly significant event since Ueshiba had heretofore refused to perform in public. This was true of all the old masters. When Funakoshi's son Gigo was sent back to Okinawa to learn a special *kata*, the teacher there would not begin instruction until all the dojo windows were firmly shuttered. Hakudo Nakayama likewise practiced his special sword techniques at four o'clock in the morning in a pitch black dojo to prevent anyone from stealing his secrets.

Kisshomaru convinced his father otherwise, telling him that people needed to see the graceful efficacy of aikido in the flesh, and thereafter Ueshiba's dramatic performances became a highlight of many an aikido demonstration. Unlike Kano and Funakoshi, of whom precious little live footage was taken, a number of films were made of Ueshiba in action, including an elaborate production shot as far back as 1935. In 1958 Ueshiba starred in a documentary entitled "Rendez-vous with Adventure," filmed by two U.S. cameramen, and he was further featured on a documentary filmed in 1961 by NHK, the Japanese national television network.

Ueshiba loved to travel, and he enjoyed visiting the newly established branch dojo in various parts of Japan. For his disciples, however, traveling with Ueshiba, both before and after the war, was the ultimate trial. His attendant for the trip could not relax for a second, and he could take nothing for granted. Ueshiba, for example, insisted on being at the train station at least an hour prior to his scheduled departure. On occasion he would refuse to board the train because "something did not feel right." Or the attendant, loaded down with gear and responsible for purchasing all the tickets, would have to play tag with the headstrong and fleet-footed aikido master, who not infrequently took off in whatever direction he wanted, regardless of the intended destination, vanishing among throngs of people.

Ueshiba had another peculiar habit of spending every single *yen* he had been given before reaching his destination. His patient wife would give the attendant enough money to cover the cost of the train tickets, refreshment, miscellaneous expenses, and a reserve for emergencies. Ueshiba somehow knew exactly how much money the attendant was carrying, and invariably stopped off at various shrines along the way to make a donation. By the end of the journey all the was gone.

One day Ueshiba visited a newly constructed shrine. He told his attendant to prepare an offering. After a moment of silent prayer, however, he turned to the attendant and said, "Keep the money. There is no god here." This particular shrine, in fact, had been constructed purely as a tourist attraction, and it had no organic, spiritual link to the site.

In 1961 Ueshiba traveled to Hawaii to inaugurate the Honolulu Aikikai Dojo. He stayed in the islands for forty days, teaching and brushing calligraphy for the local practitioners. He loved Hawaii, but told his students, "The chemicals poured on the pineapple fields here are ruining the environment. Try to get the plantation owners to stop."

Compared to the frenetic activity and continual excitement of the prewar period, Ueshiba's final years were peaceful—dedicated to study, prayer, and training. Here are some of Ueshiba's last teachings on aikido:

Aikido is medicine for a sick world. There is evil and disorder in the world because people have forgotten that all things emanate from one source. Return to that source and leave behind self-centered thoughts, petty desires, and anger.

As soon as you concern yourself with the "good" and "bad" of your fellows, you create an opening in your heart for maliciousness to enter. Testing, competing with, and criticizing others weakens and defeats you.

Your mind should be in harmony with the functioning of the universe; your body should be in tune with the movement of the universe; body and mind should be bound as one, unified with the activity of the universe.

There are no contests in aikido. A true warrior is invincible because he or she contests with nothing. "Defeat" means to defeat the mind of contention that we harbor within.

Techniques employ four qualities that reflect the nature of our world. Depending on the circumstance, your movements should be hard as a diamond, flexible as a willow, smooth-flowing like water, or as empty as space.

Calligraphy by Ueshiba: "Heavenly love." The brushwork is idio-syncratic, mysterious, inimitable—just like Ueshiba himself.

Aikido master Morihei Ueshiba, sage and wonder-worker, not long
before his death in 1969 at age eighty-six.

•

•

Near the end of his life, Ueshiba assumed an ethereal, phantom-like appearance, dressed in white robes and sporting white hair and a flowing white beard. His health gradually declined, but even when bedridden with his final illness Ueshiba was still able to summon up a miraculous cosmic force that would send four attendants flying if they started treating him as if he were nothing more than a sick old man. Like Funakoshi, Ueshiba continued to run though the techniques of his art even on his deathbed. The master of aikido passed away on April 26, 1969, aged eighty-six. Ueshiba's final instructions to his disciples were: "Aikido is for the entire world. It is not for selfish or destructive purposes. Train unceasingly for the good of all."

The Three Budo Masters Compared

I T IS OFTEN SAID THAT COMPARISONS ARE ODIOUS, but nonetheless I would like to conclude *Three Budo Masters* by drawing parallels and exploring the differences between Jigoro Kano, Gichin Funakoshi, and Morihei Ueshiba.

Physically speaking, Kano was the tallest at about 5'4". Ueshiba was a bit under 5'2", and Funakoshi was maybe 5'. In their prime, all three were built like tanks, and according to their disciples, each seemed considerably bigger in his training uniform. Health-wise, Kano had trouble with his legs later on in life, and he also suffered from diabetes. Funakoshi was quite proud that he had never been ill a day in his adult life, and had never consulted a doctor or even taken a pill. He lived the longest of the three, nearly reaching the age of ninety. Despite his reputation as a superman, Ueshiba's health was fragile, even precarious, much of his life. He may have contracted some chronic illness during his trips to Mongolia, or destroyed his digestion by engaging in a saltwater drinking contest when he was at Ayabe. Or his frequent illnesses may have been caused by his hypersensitivity. Ueshiba eventually died of liver cancer.

Regarding diet, Kano had the most eclectic tastes, eating just about anything—he especially loved beef steak— and he usually finished his long, demanding days with a nightcap. Funakoshi followed a more traditional diet of rice, vegetables, and fish, and he would rarely drink alcohol. Ueshiba's diet was primarily vegetarian but now and then included fish or chicken. He stopped drinking completely by his mid-fifties. None of the men smoked.

Let us now consider the three men as martial artists. Although formidable by any standard, Kano was probably the least technically proficient of the three. While he continued to do research on budo throughout his life, Kano in fact only trained full-time for about ten years, and he largely retired from active participation in practice around age thirty. Both Funakoshi and Ueshiba, on the other hand, had been training day and night for thirty years by the time they settled in Tokyo in their mid-fifties, and they continued personally to lead training sessions well into their eighties. Kano was aware of his limitations as a martial artist, and the open-minded and inquiring judo master had no qualms about having his students learn from both Funakoshi and Ueshiba.

Kano was much more than a martial artist, of course. Owing to his intelligence, language ability, worldwide travels, and his outstanding career as an educator, Kano was perhaps the best-informed Japanese of his era. He was certainly an inspiring example of the perfect gentlemen: impeccably mannered, deeply learned, and strong of body. Both Funakoshi and Ueshiba had the greatest respect for Kano, and never forgot his kind support of their initial efforts in Tokyo.

Even among karate exponents, Funakoshi could not have been described unequivocally as the "best." Funakoshi's greatest accomplishment was not technical superiority; rather it is was the remarkable achievement of establishing the art of karate as a noble discipline with a solid ethical base. Lacking the advantage of inherited wealth that blessed Kano and Ueshiba, and burdened with the disadvantage of being a "foreigner" in Japan's capital city, Funakoshi's fervent dedication to his art was truly impressive, and he is justly admired as the "father" of international karate.

As a martial artist, Ueshiba was in a league of his own. He was likely the greatest master ever to appear in Japan (or elsewhere). The feats of even the most legendary warriors of the past pale in comparison to Ueshiba's astonishing powers, witnessed and attested to by hundreds of people and captured on film.

Ueshiba's approach to budo was much different from that of Kano and Funakoshi. Kano's approach was thoroughly modern, and he prided himself on the rational, scientific principles of Kodokan Judo. He was not at all religious, and there was not even a Shinto shrine in the Kodokan Dojo until placement of such a shrine was mandated by nationalist bureaucrats in the 1920s. Funakoshi, too, maintained, "There is nothing mysterious about karate; no karate practitioner can exceed the natural bounds of human power." Ueshiba, though, was a shaman

•

135

•

and wonderworker who appeared to have precisely such superhuman powers.

While both Kano and Funakoshi were careful to present their teachings in a rational manner, Ueshiba functioned in a different dimension, and it was impossible to grasp intellectually what he did or said. Kano and Funakoshi prepared well-planned and thorough syllabi of study; Ueshiba never did anything the same way twice. Each day's instruction was different from the day before. By emphasizing the mystical and numinous aspects of budo, Ueshiba may have been protesting in particular against the trend to see budo as a mere physical activity (or worse, just a sport) and against the increasing materialism of contemporary society in general. Ueshiba often told his students, "Aikido is the study of the spirit! The divine has no limits!"

Since the teachings of Kano and Funakoshi were more down-to-earth, it was easier for most students to get grounded first in judo and karate. Nearly all of Ueshiba's disciples did, in fact, have extensive backgrounds in either judo or karate, or both, prior to studying with him.

Among the three masters themselves, there was not a great deal of conscious technical exchange. Kano incorporated some of Funakoshi's karate movement into a Kodokan exercise (*kime-no-kata*), but he was unable to directly borrow much from Ueshiba since their approaches were so different. There is one picture of Ueshiba in *Budo* (#67) that looks just like a karate stance, and in *Karate-Do Nyumon* the *kawashi* movements (pp. 109–13) look remarkably similar to the *irimi-tenkan* turns of aikido. Actually, it was among the students of the three budo masters that the greatest cross-fertilization took place.

Kenji Tomiki (1900–1979) was a top student of both Kano and Ueshiba, and he taught judo and aikido for many years. He even tried to combine the two, albeit without very satisfactory results and against the express wishes of Ueshiba. Minoru Mochizuki (b. 1907), another martial artist who trained under both Kano and Ueshiba, developed a composite budo system that includes elements of judo, karate, and aikido. Yasuhiro Konishi (1894–1983) and Shigeru Enami (1912–81), two of Funakoshi's principal disciples, were highly influenced by Ueshiba, and the systems they formulated were essentially aiki-karate.

It may be argued that all true masters end up practicing aikido regardless of the discipline—movements naturally become more circular, and there is more reliance on timing, *ki* power, and pure concentration than on physical strength and mechanical technique. In a sense, Ueshiba's aikido may be viewed as the culmination and fruition of budo: the outer forms of aikido can be practiced alone, with a partner, in groups, with or without weapons, as judo or karate movements. The inner forms of aikido can utilize just about any spiritual principle: Shamanism, Shintoism, Buddhism, Tantra, Christianity, Sufism, or Quantum Physics. As Ueshiba wrote, "Absorb venerable traditions into aikido by clothing them with fresh garments, and build on classic styles to create better forms."

•

•

Further Reading

In Japanese, the entire range of Kano's multifarious activities is covered in exhaustive detail by *Kano Jigoro Taikei* (The Complete Works of Jigoro Kano), issued in fifteen volumes by the Kodokan and published by Hon-no-Yusha (Tokyo, 1988). In English, there is *Kodokan Judo*, authored by Jigoro Kano, and published by Kodansha International (Tokyo, 1986). Given Kano's importance in the modernization of Japan (10,000 people attended his funeral in 1938), his role as *de facto* Foreign Minister of the country for nearly forty years, and his important part in the international Olympic movement, it is surprising that there is so little information available on him in Western languages.

Kodansha International has also published three books in English by Funakoshi: *Karate-Do Kyohan* (1975); *Karate-do: My Way of Life* (1975); and *Karate-Do Nyumon* (1988). (The Japanese editions of these books are out of print; Funakoshi's work is far more readily available in English translation than in the Japanese original.) Funakoshi's autobiography is essential reading, but since it

•

•

was written when he was in his eighties his memory had faded and he had forgotten the correct details of many events and dates. For example, in the book it states that upon deciding to stay in Tokyo and spread karate on the mainland he wrote to, and received approval from, his teachers Azato and Itosu back in Okinawa. However, at that time (1922) both men had been dead for some years. *Shotokan Karate: Its History & Evolution* by Randall G. Hassell (Focus Publications: St. Louis, Mo., 1991) and *Training with Funakoshi* by Clive Layton (Kime Publishing: Hunstanton, Norfork, England, 1992) are informative studies, and *Okinawan Karate* by Mark Bishop (A & C Black: London, 1989) gives an interesting overview of present-day karate in Okinawa.

Two biographies of Morihei Ueshiba have been written in Japanese: *Bu no shinjin* (True Man of Martial Valor) by Omoto-kyo believer Kanemoto Sunadomari (Tama Publishing: Tokyo, 1969); and *Aikido kaiso Ueshiba Morihei den* (Founder of Aikido: The Biography of Morihei Ueshiba) by Morihei's son Kisshomaru Ueshiba (Kodansha: Tokyo, 1977). K. Ueshiba also produced an illustrated biography of his father: *Aikido kaiso* (Founder of Aikido) published by Kodansha in 1983. *Aikido Shugyo* (Aikido Training) by Gozo Shioda (Takeuchi Shoten Shinsha: Tokyo, 1991) contains the eyewitness account of Ueshiba's "Firing Squad Showdown" (pp. 189–94). A full-length biography of Ueshiba in English is *Invincible Warrior* (originally published as *Abundant Peace*) by John Stevens (Shambhala Publications: Boston, 1995). Two other essential works on Ueshiba in English are *Budo:*

Teachings of the Founder of Aikido (Kodansha International: Tokyo, 1991) and *The Essence of Aikido: Spiritual Teachings of Morihei Ueshiba* (Kodansha International, 1993). See also *The Art of Peace* by Morihei Ueshiba (Shambhala Publications: Boston, 1992) and *The Secrets of Aikido* by John Stevens (Shambhala Publications, 1995).

Nihon Kakutogi Omoshiro Shiwa (Interesting Tales of Japanese Martial Artists) by Kozo Kaku (Tokyo: Mainichi Shimbunsha, 1993) contains numerous anecdotes relating to Kano, Funakoshi, Ueshiba, and their respective disciples. The Japanese journal *Hiden* (Secret Transmission), published bimonthly in Tokyo (Shibuya-ku, Sasatsuka 2-1-10-510, Tokyo 151 Japan), features many thoroughly researched articles on the three Budo masters and the historical development of Kodokan Judo, karate, and aikido. *The Fighting Spirit of Japan* by E. J. Harrison (Woodstock, N.Y.: The Overlook Press, 1983) focuses on the early years of Kodokan Judo and its relationship to jujutsu and includes a brief chapter on karate and aikido.

INDEX